NATHAN BEDFORD FORREST
& THE BATTLE OF FORT PILLOW

Yankee Myth, Confederate Fact

✒ THE LOCHLAINN SEABROOK COLLECTION ✒

Five-Star Books & Gifts From the Heart of the American South

NATHAN BEDFORD FORREST

and the Battle of

FORT PILLOW

Yankee Myth, Confederate Fact

EXCERPTED FROM THE AUTHOR'S BOOK *A REBEL BORN: A DEFENSE OF NATHAN BEDFORD FORREST*, WITH ADDITIONAL NEW MATERIAL & ILLUSTRATIONS

LOCHLAINN SEABROOK

JEFFERSON DAVIS HISTORICAL GOLD MEDAL WINNER

LAVISHLY ILLUSTRATED
EXTENSIVELY RESEARCHED

Sea Raven Press, Nashville, Tennessee, USA

NATHAN BEDFORD FORREST & THE BATTLE OF FORT PILLOW

Published by
Sea Raven Press, Cassidy Ravensdale, President
The Literary Wing of the Pro-South Movement
PO Box 1484, Spring Hill, Tennessee 37174-1484 USA
SeaRavenPress.com • searavenpress@gmail.com

Sea Raven Press

Enlightening, educational, & entertaining books for the whole family!

First Sea Raven Press paperback edition: November 2015
ISBN: 978-1-943737-10-9
Library of Congress Control Number: 2015957404

NATHAN BEDFORD FORREST AND THE BATTLE OF FORT PILLOW: YANKEE MYTH, CONFEDERATE FACT,
BY LOCHLAINN SEABROOK. INCLUDES AN INDEX, ENDNOTES, AND BIBLIOGRAPHICAL REFERENCES.

Front and back cover design and art, book design, layout, and interior art by Lochlainn Seabrook.
All images, graphic design, graphic art, and illustrations copyright © Lochlainn Seabrook.
Cover illustration: "Forrest Leading an Attack," Frank Earl Klepper
Cover illustration manipulation and design copyright © Lochlainn Seabrook.
Portions of this book have been adapted from the author's other works

The views on the American "Civil War" documented in this book are those of the publisher.

The paper used in this book is acid-free and lignin-free. It has been certified by the Sustainable Forestry
Initiative and the Forest Stewardship Council and meets all ANSI standards for archival quality paper.

PRINTED & MANUFACTURED IN OCCUPIED TENNESSEE, FORMER CONFEDERATE STATES OF AMERICA

DEDICATION

To the valorous Confederates who
fought at the Battle of Fort Pillow.

EPIGRAPH

"Nathan Bedford Forrest was born
a soldier as men are born poets."

Confederate General Dabney H. Maury

CONTENTS

SEA RAVEN PRESS

THE WORLD'S #1 SOUTH-FRIENDLY BOOK PUBLISHER

Restoring Dixie's honor
Defending traditional Southern culture
Preserving authentic Confederate history
One book at a time!

Nashville, Tennessee

SeaRavenPress.com

Notes To The Reader

THE TWO MAIN POLITICAL PARTIES IN 1860

☞ In any study of America's antebellum, bellum, and postbellum periods, it is vitally important to understand that in 1860 the two major political parties—the Democrats and the newly formed Republicans—were the opposite of what they are today. In other words, the Democrats of the mid 19th Century were Conservatives, akin to the Republican Party of today, while the Republicans of the mid 19th Century were Liberals, akin to the Democratic Party of today.

Thus the Confederacy's Democratic president, Jefferson Davis, was a Conservative (with libertarian leanings); the Union's Republican president, Abraham Lincoln, was a Liberal (with socialistic leanings).

The author's cousin, Confederate Vice President and Democrat Alexander H. Stephens: a Southern Conservative.

This is why, in the mid 1800s, the conservative wing of the Democratic Party was known as "the States' Rights Party."[1]

Hence, the Democrats of the Civil War period referred to themselves as "conservatives," "confederates," "anti-centralists," or "constitutionalists" (the latter because they favored strict adherence to the original Constitution—which tacitly guaranteed states' rights—as created by the Founding Fathers), while the Republicans called themselves "liberals," "nationalists," "centralists," or "consolidationists" (the latter three because they wanted to nationalize the central government and consolidate political power in Washington, D.C.).[2]

Since this idea is new to most of my readers, let us further demystify it by viewing it from the perspective of the American Revolutionary War. If Davis and his conservative Southern constituents (the Democrats of 1861) had been alive in 1775, they would have sided with George Washington and the American colonists, who sought to secede from the tyrannical government of Great Britain; if Lincoln and his Liberal Northern constituents (the Republicans of 1861) had been alive at that time, they would have sided with King George III and the English monarchy, who sought to maintain the American colonies as possessions of the British Empire. It is due to this very comparison that Southerners often refer to the "Civil War" as the Second American Revolutionary War.

THE TERM "CIVIL WAR"
☞ As I heartily dislike the phrase "Civil War," its use throughout this book (as well as in my other works) is worthy of an explanation.

Today America's entire literary system refers to the conflict of 1861 using the Northern term the "Civil War," whether we in the South like it or not. Thus, as all book searches by readers, libraries, and retail outlets are now performed online, and as all bookstores categorize works from this period under the heading "Civil War," book publishers and authors who deal with this particular topic have little choice but to use this term themselves. If I were to refuse to use it, as some of my Southern colleagues have suggested, few people would ever find or read my books.

Add to this the fact that scarcely any non-Southerners have ever heard of the names we in the South use for the conflict, such as the "War for Southern Independence"—or my personal preference, "Lincoln's War." It only makes sense then to use the term "Civil War" in most commercial situations.

We should also bear in mind that while today educated persons, particularly educated Southerners, all share an abhorrence for the phrase "Civil War," it was not always so. Confederates who lived through and even fought in the conflict regularly used the term throughout the 1860s, and even long after. Among them were Confederate generals such as Nathan Bedford Forrest, Richard Taylor, and Joseph E. Johnston, not to mention the Confederacy's vice president, Alexander H. Stephens.

In 1895 Confederate General James Longstreet wrote about his military experiences in a work subtitled, *Memoirs of the Civil War in America*. Even the Confederacy's highest leader, President Jefferson Davis, used the term "Civil War,"[3] and in one case at least, as late as 1881—the year he wrote his brilliant exposition, *The Rise and Fall of the Confederate Government*.[4]

A WORD ON VICTORIAN MATERIAL

☛ In order to retain the authentic historicity of the War period, I have retained the original spellings, formatting, and punctuation of the 19th-Century individuals I quote. These include such items as British-English spellings, long-running paragraphs, and other literary devices peculiar to the time.

TO LEARN MORE

☛ Lincoln's War on the American people and the Constitution can ever be fully understood without a thorough knowledge of the South's perspective. As this book's focus (Forrest and the Battle of Fort Pillow) is quite narrow, and thus only provides a brief introductory guide to these topics, one cannot hope to learn the whole truth about them here. For those who are interested in a more in-depth study, please see my comprehensive histories, listed on page 2.

For a full treatment of Forrest's fascinating life story see my biography, *A Rebel Born: A Defense of Nathan Bedford Forrest*, from which much of *Nathan Bedford Forrest and the Battle of Fort Pillow* is extracted.

THE NORTH IS STILL LYING ABOUT LINCOLN'S WAR

If Forrest were alive today, would those who now ridicule, slander, and denigrate the powerful, 6' 2", gun-toting, knife-wielding mountaineer dare say these things to his face? What do you think?

INTRODUCTION

If enemies of the South were truly interested in the facts surrounding the so-called "massacre" at Fort Pillow on April 12, 1864, they would have long ago halted their investigation into it. The truth has been widely known, published, and thoroughly examined thousands of times by some of the brightest minds in America over the past 150 years. Their conclusion has always been the same: there was no "massacre" that day and Forrest himself is guiltless, vindicated by the testimonies of both credible Northern and trustworthy Southern eyewitnesses.

Of course, South-loathers will never cease discussing, embellishing, redacting, rewriting, and retelling the tall tale of the "Butcher of Fort Pillow" and his alleged atrocities that Spring day. But this is not because they are interested in getting at the facts, for facts are nothing but a nuisance and an embarrassment to the anti-South movement. This is why they redact, revise, and rewrite history, editing and suppressing everything that does not match their liberal ideologies.

The real motivation behind the Left's endless inquiry into what it falsely calls "the most controversial battle" of Lincoln's War is twofold: 1) to continue its long tradition of punishing and shaming the South for daring to break away from the Union in 1861, and 2) to humiliate both Forrest and the Southern people for being conservative, traditional, and religious. The Left is, after all, liberal, progressive, and atheistic.

May the facts recorded in this little book aid in the repudiation of the anti-South propaganda fabricated by the Liberal establishment; and may they help preserve the honor and memory of the brave Confederate soldiers who served, fought, and died at Henning, Tennessee, on April 12, 1864, in the South's never-ending struggle for constitutional freedom. It continues today, and as a Southern writer and a descendant of Confederate soldiers, I am proud to be part of it.

Liberals will go on arguing amongst themselves. However, as a Southerner I consider this book, along with the General's postwar exoneration by the U.S. government, to be the final word on the matter of the Battle of Fort Pillow. God bless Ol' Bedford and God bless Dixie.

Lochlainn Seabrook
Nashville, Tennessee, USA
November 2015

Map of the Battle of Fort Pillow, April 12, 1864, Henning, Tennessee

1
RIGHTING THE ERRORS
OF YANKEE MYTHOLOGY

INTRODUCTION

AT THE BATTLE OF FORT Pillow, Tennessee, April 12, 1864, Confederate General Nathan Bedford Forrest achieved one of his most stunning triumphs. Sadly, in the ongoing effort to malign his good name, obscure the Confederate victory, and maintain support for Lincoln's illegal assault on the South, Yankee mythographers quickly invented the story that a "racist massacre" had taken place. Within days the tale had taken on a life of its own, each storyteller adding his own lurid details and embellishments of incidents that never occurred in real life; only in the minds of their inventors.

Nathan Bedford Forrest during the War.

In 1864, for instance, only months after the battle, Thomas L. Wilson wrote one of the most virulent, anti-South pieces of propaganda ever published: *Sufferings Endured For a Free Government: A History of the Cruelties and Atrocities of the Rebellion.* Though the author could not even grasp that it was the South, not the North, that was fighting for a "free government," his Yankee-slanted book purports to provide the authentic facts of "the Confederacy's many war crimes," not the least of which was the "massacre" at Fort Pillow. Wrote Wilson of Forrest and his men:

. . . [there] followed a scene of cruelty and murder without parallel in civilized warfare, which needed but the tomahawk and scalping-knife to exceed the worst atrocities ever committed by savages. The rebels commenced an indiscriminate slaughter, sparing neither age nor sex, white or black, soldier or civilian. The officers and men seemed to vie with each other in the devilish work. Men and women, and even children, wherever found, were deliberately shot down, beaten, and hacked with sabres. Some of the children, not more than ten years old, were forced to stand up and face their murderers while being shot. The sick and wounded were butchered without mercy, the rebels even entering the hospital-building and dragging them out to be shot, or killing them as they lay there unable to offer the least resistance. All over the hillside the work of murder was going on. Numbers of our men were collected together in lines or groups and deliberately shot. Some were shot while in the river, while others on the bank were shot and their bodies kicked into the water, many of them still living, but unable to make any exertions to save themselves from drowning. Some of the rebels stood upon the top of the hill, or a short distance down its side, and called to our soldiers to come up to them—and as they approached, shot them down in cold blood: if their guns or pistols missed fire, forcing them to stand there until they were again prepared to fire. All around were heard cries of "No quarter! no quarter! kill the damned niggers, shoot them down!" All who asked for mercy were answered by the most cruel taunts and sneers. Some were spared for a time, only to be murdered under circumstances of greater cruelty.[5]

This preposterous anecdote does not have the ring of truth. Yet it is presented as historical fact, one more of a long line of Northern attempts to besmirch the South and permanently mar Forrest's reputation.

Another example came in 1867, when African-American author and abolitionist William Wells Brown devoted an entire chapter of his book, *The Negro in the American Rebellion*, to "The Massacre at Fort Pillow." The chapter begins with these fantastic words:

Nothing in the history of the Rebellion has equalled in inhumanity and atrocity the horrid butchery at Fort Pillow, Ky., on the 13th of April, 1864. In no other school than slavery could human beings have been trained to such readiness for cruelties like these. Accustomed to brutality and bestiality all their lives, it was easy for them to perpetrate the atrocities which will startle the civilized foreign world, as they have awakened the indignation of our own people [that is, African-Americans].[6]

That Brown's version is based on faulty fictions fabricated by biased individuals who knew nothing about the actual conflict is obvious: the date he gives for the battle, as well as the state in which he says it took place, are both incorrect. Priming his audience for the anti-South propaganda that is to come, the author asserts that such outrages could have only been committed by slavery-loving Southern whites who were "accustomed to brutality and bestiality all their lives." No mention that American slavery started in the North, that the American abolition movement was born in the South, that up until the late 1700s the North had many more slaves than the South, that tens of thousands of American blacks also owned slaves, or that the South was well-known for being far more civilized and racially tolerant than the North.[7]

"McCulloch's men taking the first line of fortification" at the Battle of Fort Pillow.

According to Wilson, Brown, and their fellow Dixie-hating brethren, Northern blacks (and whites) were allegedly captured, tortured, and crucified, or were gunned down during the act of surrender at Fort Pillow. Other reports claimed that Confederates had buried and burned wounded Union soldiers alive, and that theft of the injured and the dead took place under cover of darkness the night of the battle. One of the more notorious and absurd accusations was that

Forrest executed captured Union officer Major William F. Bradford.

In 1887 another writer, William T. Alexander, devotes a section of his book, *History of the Colored Race in America*, to the Confederates' supposed "carnival of murder" at Fort Pillow:

> . . . the [Yankee] garrison, throwing down their arms, fled down the steep bank, trying to hide behind trees or logs, or skulk in bushes, or find comparative safety in the river. The Confederates followed, butchering white and colored soldiers and non-combatants, men, women and children, with no more discrimination than humanity.
>
> Disabled men were made to stand up and then be shot; others were burned with the tents wherein they had been nailed to the floor. This carnival of murder continued till dark, and was even renewed the next morning. Major Bradford was not murdered till they had taken him as a prisoner several miles on their retreat South.
>
> It was in vain that Forrest and his superior officer undertook to palliate this infernal atrocity in defiance of their own record.[8]

Long afterward Union officers used these Yankee fairy tales to inspire vengeance in their troops. One who experienced this "inspiration" firsthand was Dr. Moses Greeley Parker, a surgeon with the Fifty-seventh Massachusetts Regiment. At the start of a Federal attack on a Confederate stronghold in Virginia, the unit's officer, Captain Dollard, shouted out: "Remember Fort Pillow!" "The work was short," Parker later recalled, "not one Confederate soldier was left to tell the tale."[9] The Yanks thus used a fake massacre to commit a real one!

Countering all of this nonsense were the bonafide reports of Confederate soldiers who were actually present at the Battle of Fort Pillow. Among them was Sergeant Richard R. Hancock of Company C, Second Tennessee Cavalry. In 1887 Hancock cited the book *The Campaigns of General Nathan Bedford Forrest*: after Forrest's troops withdrew from the area,

> there remained at Fort Pillow none save the [Confederate] dead who had fallen in storming it, and the [Union] dead of the late garrison, victims, not of unlawful acts of war, as has been so virulently alleged and generally believed at the North, but of an

insensate endeavor, as foolishly resolved as feebly executed, to hold
a position naturally untenable and badly fortified; victims, we may
add, of the imbecility and grievous mismanagement of those weak,
incapable officers whom the fortunes of war unhappily had placed
over them.[10]

Despite the many authentic testimonies of eyewitnesses like
Hancock, nothing could stop the Yankee propaganda machine once it
began rolling. Even Union President Abraham Lincoln got in on the act
of whitewashing authentic history. When his Yankee constituency began
demanding retribution for Forrest's alleged crimes at the fort, the
Northern chief executive felt compelled to respond. On April 18, 1864,
he made the following public remarks at Baltimore, Maryland, promising
retaliation if the scuttlebutt turned out to be true:

> A painful rumor—true, I fear—has reached us of the massacre by
> the rebel forces at Fort Pillow, in the west end of Tennessee, on
> the Mississippi River, of some three hundred colored soldiers and
> white officers, who had just been overpowered by their assailants.
> . . . We do not to-day know that a colored soldier, or
> white officer commanding colored soldiers, has been massacred by
> the rebels when made a prisoner. We fear it,—believe it, I may
> say,—but we do not know it. To take the life of one of their
> prisoners on the assumption that they murder ours, when it is short
> of certainty that they do murder ours, might be too serious, too
> cruel, a mistake. We are having the Fort Pillow affair thoroughly
> investigated; and such investigation will probably show conclusively
> how the truth is. If after all that has been said it shall turn out that
> there has been no massacre at Fort Pillow, it will be almost safe to
> say there has been none, and will be none, elsewhere. If there has
> been the massacre of three hundred there, or even the tenth part of
> three hundred, it will be conclusively proved; and being so proved,
> the retribution shall as surely come. It will be matter of grave
> consideration in what exact course to apply the retribution; but in
> the supposed case it must come.[11]

The ridiculous Yankee fables surrounding Fort Pillow were later
enlarged and reenforced by the North's overtly slanted Wade-Gooch
Report (issued on May 5, 1864), headed by two extreme radical South-
haters: Senator Benjamin F. Wade and Representative Daniel W. Gooch.
The paper asserted, among other things, that Forrest and his men had

intentionally shot down surrendering pro-Union Tennesseans and former slaves-turned-soldiers during the battle—even though it was obvious then as it is now that this was a bald-faced lie: not a single Yank at the scene ever surrendered.[12] Why? Because their commander Major Bradford told them not to.[13] With such facts at hand, even many Northerners admitted that the report was one of the finest examples of anti-South disinformation and propaganda produced during the War.[14]

Ohio Senator Benjamin F. Wade.

This was the only time during his entire military career that Forrest was accused of cruelty and inhumane conduct toward prisoners,[15] this fact alone making it highly suspect. Because of the seriousness of these charges, and because his critics maintain that his worst traits (allegedly racism, sadism, and dishonesty) were exhibited here, a detailed examination of this episode will be beneficial in revealing the facts about the General and Fort Pillow.[16]

RESISTANCE WAS FUTILE

The truth, from Forrest's own lips, is that if any Union soldiers were killed after the assault, it was only because they continued to shoot *and* resist surrendering.[17] As he did during most of the conflicts at which he was commander, Forrest had sent out a flag of truce along with a demand of surrender to the enemy at Fort Pillow, with the promise that *all* those captured, both white and black, would be treated as prisoners of war. The purpose? As always, "to prevent the further effusion of blood."[18] His dispatch read:

> HEADQUARTERS CONFEDERATE CAVALRY, NEAR FORT PILLOW
> April 12, 1864.
> Major [Lionel F.] Booth, Commanding U. S. Forces, Fort Pillow:
> MAJOR: The conduct of the officers and men garrisoning Fort Pillow has been such as to entitle them to being treated as prisoners of war. I demand the unconditional surrender of the entire garrison, promising that you shall be treated as prisoners of war.

My men have just received a fresh supply of ammunition, and from their present position can easily assault and capture the fort. Should my demand be refused, I cannot be responsible for the fate of your command.

Respectfully, N. B. FORREST, Major-General, Commanding. [19]

Unwisely, the demand was ignored, with the tragic results, as we will explore shortly.

What we have here, however, is proof of Forrest's good and humane intentions at the very start of the conflict. [20] No acts of cruelty were premeditated or committed. Just a simple and direct plan to capture the garrison as quickly as possible, with the least amount of fanfare and bloodshed possible. This was the "Forrest method" after all.

Indeed, for the rest of their lives the General and his men would testify under oath that no atrocities occurred, and that

all allegations to the contrary are mere malicious inventions, started, nurtured, and accredited at a time, and through a sentiment of strong sectional animosity. [21]

Anything else, they repeatedly asserted, was the product of "hysteria" and the overwrought imaginations of enemies of the South. [22] Even those Rebels not with Forrest at Fort Pillow understood what had happened there: it was the result of the irrational and resistant behavior of the Yanks at the fort, despite knowing full well that the garrison would soon be overrun and taken. [23]

The truth was that the "massacre" legend resulted largely from Northern journalists. As Forrest himself put it to his men:

They came forth with threats of vengeance towards you and your commander for the bloody victory of Fort Pillow, made a massacre only by dastardly Yankee reporters. [24]

Such statements were corroborated by others in the Confederate army. In 1879, Forrest's superior, General Richard Taylor, one of the most respected and fair-minded men of the War on either side, set the record straight. Forrest, wrote Taylor,

. . . was a tender-hearted, kindly man. The accusations of his

enemies that he murdered prisoners at Fort Pillow and elsewhere
are absolutely false. The prisoners captured on his expedition into
Tennessee . . . were negroes, and he carefully looked after their
wants himself, though in rapid movement and fighting much of the
time. These negroes told me of Mass Forrest's kindness to them.[25]

Forrest felt strongly enough about the false accusations that he
was willing to die over them. During the 1868 presidential campaign,
for example, a former Union cavalry officer named Judson Kilpatrick
gave a number of public speeches lambasting Forrest for numerous
alleged war crimes, among them Fort Pillow, where, the brazen Yankee
declared, the Rebel commander had crucified and burned blacks to
death.[26]

Forrest responded as only
Forrest could: after calling Kilpatrick
several unflattering names, and using
the local newspaper to refute the
Yankee's claims, he publically
challenged him to a duel[27] (even
though dueling was illegal).[28] After
the site, seconds, weapons, and
horses had been selected, however,
Kilpatrick came to his senses and
quickly backed out,[29] a decision that
no doubt greatly prolonged his life.[30]

The question is why would
either Forrest or Kilpatrick have
sacrificed their lives over a lie? The
answer is that they would not have.

Union General Judson Kilpatrick.

For there was no "massacre" at Fort Pillow.

Yet today, many, in particular many Southern blacks and most
white liberals, have a deep and abiding hatred for Forrest due to his
alleged role at the battle, comparing him to Jack the Ripper, Mussolini,
and even Hitler.[31]

When it comes to Fort Pillow then, who is to be believed,
Forrest and his Confederate comrades, or a highly biased, South-
loathing, Northern media? Let us briefly touch on the highlights of the
event, and allow the facts to speak for themselves.

THE YANKS' 40 PERCENT DEATH RATE

The Northern press at the time whined that the number of Union soldiers who died in the conflict, 40 percent,[32] was far above average:[33] of the 557 Yankee soldiers present (295 whites and 262 blacks), 231 were killed (226 were captured and 100 were wounded).[34]

Yet, a 40 percent death rate among the enemy is exactly what one would expect of a fort taken by assault, the type of approach used by Forrest and his men at Fort Pillow.[35] Or to put it another way, as Jordan and Pryor remark: "For a place taken by storm the loss was by no means heavy."[36]

What is more, throughout the War the mortality rate among black Union soldiers was always 40 percent higher than for white Union soldiers.[37] This was due in great part to Lincoln's unequal treatment of his black and white soldiers. Black Union soldiers, for instance, were given inferior training, weapons, ammunition, and clothing,[38] and were often used as shock troops, sent into battle first to spare white lives.[39] Thus the 40 percent figure at Fort Pillow should not be held out as a military anomaly. Rather it was the norm among black Union forces.[40]

More importantly, many of the blacks among the 40 percent who died at Fort Pillow died *before* the garrison was even attacked by Forrest (who led the main charge at about 11:00 AM)[41]—casualties of his formidable and nationally acclaimed sharpshooters,[42] whose enfilading fire power completely swept every square foot of terrain in the area that day.[43]

Yankees at the scene later verified this. In his official report, one of these, Union Adjutant Mack J. Leaming, writes:

> At 5.30 o'clock on the morning of the 12th of April, 1864, our pickets were attacked and driven in by the advance of the enemy, under command of General Forrest.[44] Our garrison immediately opened fire on the advancing rebels from our artillery at the fort, while Companies D and E, of the Thirteenth West Tennessee Cavalry [Union], were deployed as skirmishers, which duty they performed until about 8 a. m., when they were compelled to retire to the fort after considerable loss, in which Lieutenant Barr, of Company D, was killed.
> The firing continued without cessation, principally from behind logs, stumps, and under cover of thick underbrush and from high knolls, until about 9 a. m., when the rebels made a general

assault on our works, which was successfully repulsed with severe loss to them and but slight loss to our garrison. We, however, suffered pretty severely in the loss of commissioned officers by the unerring aim of the rebel sharpshooters, and among this loss I have to record the name of our post commander Maj. L. F. Booth, who was killed almost instantly by a musket-ball through the breast.[45]

History is replete with hundreds of examples of real battle massacres that occurred, whose victorious commanders have been lionized not pilloried. Yet Forrest, who led a fair and humane campaign against the Federals at Fort Pillow, continues to be excoriated.[46] Why? Because of a blind hatred of the South, along with her heroes, beliefs, traditions, and symbols.

But even if a massacre had taken place at Fort Pillow, it would have been justified, for as one writer noted shortly after Lincoln's War:

Every military man knows that whenever a place is taken by assault under the flag of any nation, many of the defenders are put to death though they throw down their arms and cry for quarter.[47]

There were numerous other factors that contributed to the 40 percent figure:[48]

• A poorly designed fort.[49]
• The loss, early in the fight, of the principle Union commander, the level-headed Major Lionel F. Booth.[50]
• Booth's replacement by the inexperienced,[51] weak, cowardly, and vain Union officer Major William F. Bradford.[52]
• The deaths of most of the commissioned Union officers *before* the Rebels even entered the fort—which left their troops ungoverned for the rest of the fight.[53]
• The Union defense of an indefensible and strategically unimportant fort[54] (something no intelligent officer would ever allow).[55]
• The Yanks' poor plan of defense, which entailed no procedure for surrender.[56]
• Widespread drunkenness among the Union soldiery,[57] which caused them to be "crazed" with "fright and intoxication."[58]
• The Yanks' refusal to surrender.[59]

- Retreat of the Union garrison without lowering their fort flag.[60]
- Confusion over the truce.[61]
- Union-sympathizing Southern civilians in the fort.[62]
- The "reckless and insane" defense of the fort by a Yankee command that was severely outnumbered and out-officered.[63]
- A complex topography.[64]
- Mass Yankee drownings.[65]
- A lack of promised U.S. naval reinforcement.[66]

The assertion that Forrest ordered a merciless slaughter of the Yankee garrison then is demonstrably false, for the particulars listed above were all quite beyond his control.[67] Indeed, it is now known with absolute certainty that he did all he could, not only to forestall any unnecessary violence, but also to check any unnecessary bloodshed.[68]

Respected British military authority General Viscount Wolseley had this to say on the topic:

> . . . I do not think the fact that about one-half of the small garrison of a place taken by assault, was either killed or wounded, evinced any very unusual bloodthirstiness on the part of the assailants.[69]

In 1902 many of Forrest's men were still alive and able to comment on the so-called "slaughter" at Fort Pillow on April 12, 1864. According to their testimony concerning the Yankee death toll and other alleged atrocities that day,

> it was not greater than the circumstances justified; . . . none were killed after they surrendered, . . . and no prisoners were killed or mistreated in or out of the fort that day or the next day.[70]

Forrest himself avowed that no gun was fired and that no Yankee prisoner was injured after the fort was captured.[71] And even if there had been any barbarities committed, on either side, these would have to be largely attributed to *insania belli* (the "insanity of war"), a terrible but inevitable aspect of all violent conflicts.[72]

It is worth repeating the words of Jordan and Pryor, who noted that those Yanks who perished at Fort Pillow were victims, not of unlawful acts of war, as has been so virulently alleged and generally believed at the North, but of an insensate endeavor, as foolishly resolved as feebly executed, to hold a position naturally untenable and badly fortified,—the victims, we may add, in all sincerity, not of a savage ferocity on the part of their late adversaries, but of the imbecility and grievous mismanagement of those weak, incapable officers, whom the fortunes of war unhappily had placed over them.[73]

WHERE WAS FORREST DURING THE "MASSACRE"?

The real question is this: was Forrest responsible for any of the purported savageries that occurred at Fort Pillow?

For one thing, he had been severely injured from a horse falling on him,[74] and was not even at the front of the lines when the alleged outrages were said to have taken place. When the fighting momentarily abated, Forrest actually tried to prevent further Yankee deaths by raising a flag of truce, which the enemy duly ignored; indeed, there was never any formal surrender on the part of the Yanks.[75]

Yanks line the fortifications at Fort Pillow.

When he finally did arrive at the front (after a five to ten minute ride),[76] Forrest immediately ordered a cease fire (later attested to by a black U.S. soldier at the scene)[77] and personally arrested a Rebel soldier who ignored the command.[78] According to one report, Forrest even killed one of his own men for refusing to give quarter to the enemy.[79] Clearly, he had gone to extraordinary lengths to prevent any unnecessary bloodshed.[80]

Forrest was then immediately forced to return to his post in the rear,[81] some 400 yards back,[82] because even though a flag of truce was flying,[83] black Yankee soldiers—many who were inebriated and making vulgar gestures and yelling obscene epithets at the Rebs[84] (so foul that they cannot be described here)[85]—were shooting off their rifles in a threatening manner.[86]

2

WHY FORREST
ATTACKED FORT PILLOW

THE MOST IMPORTANT QUESTION

ONE QUESTION FORREST'S CRITICS NEVER ask is why he
attacked this insignificant garrison to begin with.

Forrest's original intention was to shut down the fort
and its "nest of outlaws,"[87] its "lair" of white and black Yankee occupants
comprised of scallywag "wretches" and Tennessee Tories, all who had
been a menace to West Tennessee.[88] For
some period of time they had been
viciously insulting, robbing, raping,
despoiling, attacking, and generally
preying on the defenseless women,
children, and elderly living in the
surrounding counties (their sons,
brothers, and husbands were all off
fighting Lincoln's unlawful invaders).[89]

Indeed, the U.S.'s own provost
marshal records plainly show that at the
time Yankee troops were committing
untold numbers of "local genocides" across the South, executing
hundreds of Southern civilians without trial, deporting thousands of
civilians who lived near railroad lines, and routinely raping Southern
women. Also revealed in these documents is the fact that Yankee
officers were commonly using torture on Southern noncombatants.[90]

Forrest and his men had another motivation. Like other traditional Southerners, they did not recognize Lincoln's hollow, self-serving, fake Emancipation Proclamation. Why? Because Lincoln only issued it in the South, where he had no legal authority, as Dixie had become an independent nation, the Confederate States of America, in February 1861. (Revealingly, in the North Lincoln left slavery completely intact, "as if this proclamation were not issued," as his edict clearly states.)[91]

Thus Forrest and his cavalrymen viewed the blacks at Fort Pillow, some 50 percent who were runaway slaves, as "private property" that were by law supposed to be returned to their owners,[92] as the following field communication from the General to the enemy in the fall of 1864 proves:

> HEADQUARTERS FORREST'S CAVALRY,
> In the Field, September 24, 1864.
> *Officer Commanding U. S. Forces, Athens, Alabama:*
> I demand an immediate and unconditional surrender of the entire force and all government stores and property at this post. I have a sufficient force to storm and take your works, and if I am forced to do so the responsibility of the consequences must rest with you. Should you, however, accept the terms, all white soldiers shall be treated as prisoners of war and the negroes returned to their masters. A reply is requested immediately. Respectfully,
> N. B. Forrest, Major-General C. S. Army.[93]

We will note here that blacks were still considered "contraband" in the North at this time, a dehumanizing term never used by the South for her black servants, and one that proves that most Yankees still viewed blacks as little more than servile pieces of property in 1864. Forrest himself stated that the treatment of captured black soldiers was not a personal matter determined by individual officers, but was decided by the C.S. and the U.S. governments, and was thus out of his hands.[94]

In short, Forrest's policy concerning captured blacks was, as he so often reiterated, not to kill them, but to "handle them well and return them to their owners . . . ."[95] As slavery was still protected by both the U.S. Constitution and the C.S. Constitution at the time, this alone was full justification for launching an attack on Fort Pillow.

The fact is that the Union force at the fort had no official business being there: in addition to preying on the local populace, this small group of Yanks had set up a trading post at the site, originally a Confederate fort (and as such the property of the Confederate state of Tennessee), for their own financial gain. Sherman later said that he did not know Federal forces occupied the fort, and that it was not even on his list of garrisons.[96]   Indeed, he had earlier ordered it to be abandoned.[97] Even Lincoln would have disapproved of a Union military presence there, as it was a waste of valuable government resources.

In 1868 Jordan and Pryor described the situation this way:

Ever since his advent into West-Tennessee, Forrest had been distressed by well-authenticated instances, repeatedly brought to his notice, of rapine and atrocious outrage upon non-combatants of the country, by the [Yankee] garrison at Fort Pillow. And a delegation of the people of the town of Jackson and surrounding region now waited upon and earnestly besought him to leave a brigade for their protection against this nest of outlaws. According to the information received, the garrison in question consisted of a battalion of whites, commanded by [Union] Major Bradford, (a Tennessean,) and a negro battalion under Major Booth, who likewise commanded the post. Many of Bradford's men were known to be deserters from the Confederate army, and the rest were men of the country who entertained a malignant hatred toward Confederate soldiers, their families and friends. Under the pretense of scouring the country for arms and "rebel soldiers," Bradford and his subalterns had traversed the surrounding country with detachments, robbing the people of their horses, mules, beef cattle, beds, plate, wearing apparel, money, and every possible movable article of value, besides venting upon the wives and daughters of Southern soldiers the most opprobrious and obscene epithets, with more than one extreme outrage upon the persons of these victims of their hate and lust.

The families of many of Forrest's men had been thus grievously wronged, despoiled, and insulted, and in one or two cases fearfully outraged, and many of his officers, uniting with the citizens of the country in the petition, begged to be permitted to remain, to shield their families from further molestation. Of course this was impossible; but Forrest determined to employ his present resources for the summary suppression of the evil and grievances complained of, by the surprise, if possible, and capture, at all hazards, of Fort Pillow; and the orders necessary to that end were issued on the 10th of April; Bell's and McCulloch's Brigades, with Walton's Battery—four mountain howitzers—being selected for the operation.[98]

Forrest had one other motivation for paying a visit to Fort Pillow: "Uncle Sam's larder." As he noted on April 4, 1864:

> There is a Federal force of 500 or 600 at Fort Pillow, which I shall attend to in a day or two, as they have horses and supplies which we need.[99]

In summary, when the defenseless people of the region begged Forrest for help, the General, having nothing else pressing at the moment and needing provisions and supplies, gladly promised to relieve them of the nefarious scallywags and criminals. It was for these reasons that Forrest and his men attacked Fort Pillow, not to single out and kill blacks, as anti-South propagandists claim.[100]

FALSE CHARGES & YANKEE RACISM

Characteristically, the Yankees labeled Forrest's attack at Fort Pillow a "massacre" and an "assassination." But these were merely the usual scurrilous terms employed—out of jealousy, anger, and frustration—by the North for Confederate successes on the battlefield.[101] Even historians with no love for the South admit that the Northern media turned the truth into a fictitious tale of wanton cruelty, and that the numerical figures they used were overly and unjustly magnified.[102]

Union General
Cadwallader C. Washburn.

Besides, "playing the massacre card" was one of the vile hands the Yanks were best at dealing. Indeed, Forrest was far from being the only white Confederate accused of slaughtering blacks. For instance, Union General Cadwallader C. Washburn later slanderously and falsely charged General Stephen Dill Lee with massacring U.S. African-American soldiers at the Battle of Brice's Cross Roads—another piece of revisionist Yankee "history."[103]

As many Rebels later asserted, both the Union soldiers at the garrison and Lincoln (along with the Northern populace) should have expected what was coming. For, as just mentioned, the Fort Pillow Yanks had been committing outrages on the surrounding noncombatant populace for several months. Forrest and his men, who rightly took these crimes as personal insults, sought only to protect the innocent.[104] Yankees would have done no less to protect their own.

Of course, one thing that none of the Northern papers reported was that the white and black Union troops stationed at Fort Pillow were segregated,[105] while Forrest's white and black soldiers at the scene were integrated (segregation of troops was a type of racism unheard of in the Confederate Army, where black and whites fought together, side by side).[106]

THE FACTS
There is little question that the South won a decisive victory at Fort Pillow, and that a seemingly unusually disproportionate number of Federal soldiers died, many of them African-Americans. The question is why?

The answer that has come down to us today is part fact, part fiction; part emotion, part politics; part Forrest's ingeniousness, part Yankee stupidity. The complete story will never be known.

Nonetheless, we do have some clear facts to work with.

To begin with, a number of the Yankee soldiers, in particular many of the blacks, were thoroughly intoxicated on April 12.[107] After the battle countless barrels of whiskey and kegs of beer and ale were found scattered throughout the fort, up and down the works, with tin dippers[108] and cups tied to them for convenience,[109] as Forrest and his officers later testified.[110]

Standing defiantly on the parapets, black U.S. troops taunted, jeered, shouted obscenities, and made obscene gestures at Forrest's men, daring them to attack. In their thoroughly inebriated state they apparently felt immortal and refused to obey Forrest's usual command to "surrender or die." Unaware at the time that the Federals were drunk, and observing their staunch resistance, Forrest gave his usual order to "shoot at everything blue betwixt wind and water until yonder flag comes down."[111] His soldiers rightfully proceeded to unfurl a galling and murderous fire upon them, and dozens fell.[112]

This incident only explains some of the Union injuries and deaths, however. In fact, there was another factor behind the hundreds of Yankee casualties, one that can be better understood by examining the enthusiasm with which Forrest's men attacked.

YANKEE CRIMES AGAINST FORREST'S MEN, RELATIONS, FRIENDS, & NEIGHBORS

Prior to the Battle of Fort Pillow, the Yankee soldiers who manned that garrison (many themselves, like Forrest's men, also from Tennessee) were known to have captured, tortured, and murdered individuals from Forrest's cavalry.

At least seven of Forrest's men died in this manner, though only six are known. We record their names here for posterity: Lieutenant Joseph Stewart, Private John Wilson, Private Samuel Osborn (all three "shot to death"), Private Martin (first name unknown; "shot to death"), Lieutenant Willis Dodds (illegally arrested at his father's house and "put to death by [mutilation and] torture"), and Private Alexander Vale ("shot to death"). The seventh victim, while still alive, was horribly mutilated by Yankees and left to die. Suffering a most appalling death, the details of his unspeakable agonies and numerous wounds are too gruesome to recount here.

Nathan Bedford Forrest.

These heinous crimes made it into the United States' *Official Records*, there for all to see, read, study, and ponder. One of the primary Yankee villains behind these murders was Colonel Fielding Hurst, sent by another Yankee war criminal, General William Sooy Smith,[113] to "grub up" West Tennessee. If by "grub up" Smith meant that Hurst should extort, rob, torture, mutilate, and shoot unarmed Confederate soldiers as well as civilians (even "helpless," physically handicapped children), then Hurst succeeded admirably.

An outraged Forrest ordered one of his officers, Lieutenant-

Colonel Wiley M. Reed, to investigate. A month before Fort Pillow, on March 21, 1864, from his headquarters at Jackson, Forrest wrote to Confederate Lieutenant Colonel Thomas M. Jack:

> Numerous reports having reached me of the wanton destruction of property by Col. Fielding Hurst and his regiment of renegade Tennesseans, I ordered Lieut. Col. W. M. Reed to investigate and report upon the same, and herewith transmit you a copy of his report. Have thought it both just and proper to bring these transactions to the notice of the Federal commander at Memphis, and by flag of truce will demand of him the restitution of the money taken from the citizens of Jackson, under a threat from Hurst to burn the town unless the money was forthcoming at an appointed time. Have also demanded that the murderers be delivered up to Confederate authority for punishment, and reply from that officer as to the demand, &c., will be forwarded you as soon as received. Should the Federal commander refuse to accede to the just demands made, I have instructed the officer in charge of the flag to deliver the notice inclosed outlawing Hurst and his command.
> I am, general, very respectfully, your obedient servant,
> N. B. FORREST, Major-General. [114]

Dated the same day, Reed sent an official report on some of Hurst's crimes to his superior Confederate Major John P. Strange:

HEADQUARTERS FORREST'S COMMAND,
Jackson, Tenn., March 21, 1864.
Maj. J. P. STRANGE,
Assistant Adjutant-General:
MAJOR: Having been appointed by the major-general commanding to investigate the facts of the recent tax levied by Col. Fielding Hurst upon the citizens of this place to indemnify himself and command against damages assessed by the Federal authorities of Memphis in favor of Mrs. Newman, formerly a citizen of Jackson, whose house had been entered and robbed by the Federal soldiery in the summer of 1863, also the facts available in reference to the murders which have been committed by the enemy upon soldiers and citizens in this part of the State within the past few months, in obedience to instructions I called together a party of citizens, from whom I derived the following facts: About the 7th of February, 1864, Colonel Hurst, with his command, visited Jackson, Tenn., and announced publicly that in consequence of the

assessment by the Federal authorities of Memphis, Tenn., against himself and command of damages to the amount of $5,139.25 in favor of Mrs. Newman, formerly a citizen of this place, he was here to demand this amount at once of the citizens, or on refusal or failure promptly to pay said amount into his hands that he would burn the town. Upon application of some of the citizens and the guaranty of 20 of them, five days were granted in which to raise the sum required, to be paid in greenbacks or Kentucky funds. On the 12th of February, 1864, the entire amount, $5,139.25, was paid into the hands of Col. Fielding Hurst by the citizens of Jackson, Tenn.

The murders committed are as follows: Lieut. Willis Dodds, Company F, Colonel [John F.] Newsom's regiment Tennessee volunteers, Forrest's command, under orders from his commanding officers, collecting his command, was arrested at the residence of his father in Henderson County, Tenn., on or about the 9th of March, 1864, by the command of Colonel Thornburgh, of the Federal army, on their march through this portion of the State eastward, and put to death by torture.

Private Silas Hodges, a scout, acting under orders from Colonel Tansil, states that he saw the body of Lieutenant Dodds very soon after his murder, and that it was most horribly mutilated, the face having been skinned, the nose cut off, the under jaw disjointed, the privates cut off, and the body otherwise barbarously lacerated and most wantonly injured, and that his death was brought about by the most inhuman process of torture.

Private Alex. Vale, Company H, Newsom's regiment Tennessee volunteers, under orders from Colonel Tansil, was arrested and shot to death in Madison County, Tenn., by same command, on or about the 8th March, 1864.

Lieut. Joseph Stewart, Private John Wilson, Private Samuel Osborn, members of Newsom's regiment Tennessee volunteers, while on duty under orders from their commanding officers, were captured by Hurst's command on or about the 15th February, 1864, in McNairy County, Tenn., and about three days thereafter their bodies were found in Haywood County, Tenn., having been shot to death.

On or about the 5th February, 1864, Private Martin, Company—, Wilson's regiment Tennessee volunteers, was captured by same command and was shot to death and the rights of sepulture forbidden while the command remained, some four days. Mr. Lee Doroughty, a citizen of McNairy County, Tenn, a youth about sixteen years of age, deformed and almost helpless, was arrested and wantonly murdered by same command about 1st January, 1864.

I am, major, very respectfully, your obedient servant,
W. M. REED, Lieutenant-Colonel, Provisional Army, C. S.[115]

Forrest had a serious score to settle.[116] The next day he let it be known among the Yankee brass that if Hurst and his men were ever captured, they would *not* be considered prisoners of war, but rather would be treated as the common criminals they were:

> HDQRS. DEPT. OF WEST TENN. AND NORTH MISS.,
> In the Field, March 22, 1864.
> To whom it may concern:
> Whereas it has come to the knowledge of the major-general commanding that Col. Fielding Hurst, commanding [Sixth] Regiment U. S. [Tennessee Cavalry] Volunteers, has been guilty of wanton extortion upon the citizens of Jackson, Tenn., and other places, guilty of depredations upon private property, guilty of house burning, guilty of murders, both of citizens and soldiers of the Confederate States; and whereas demand has been duly made upon the military authorities of the United States for the surrender of said Col. Fielding Hurst and such officers and men of his command as are guilty of these outrages; and whereas this just demand has been refused by said authorities: I therefore declare the aforesaid Fielding Hurst, and the officers and men of his command, outlaws, and not entitled to be treated as prisoners of war falling into the hands of the forces of the Confederate States.
> N. B. FORREST, Major-General, Commanding.[117]

These were not the first or the last war crimes Union General William Sooy Smith would sanction or himself commit. In August of that same year, 1864, as he marched across Mississippi, his unlawful acts against the innocent inhabitants of Oxford spawned the following rebuke from two of Forrest's biographers, Jordan and Pryor:

> The Federal advance, however, did not enter Oxford until about eight o'clock on the morning of the 22nd, but a column of infantry soon followed. The cavalry were speedily and widely scattered through the town, but the infantry were kept in ranks. Up to noon, although there were a number of petty acts of spoliation on the part of individual soldiers, yet no general disposition was shown either to license or commit arson and rape. The railroad depot was burned in the morning, but, as yet, no private buildings were set on fire. Suddenly, about midday, however, this forbearance

ceased. Orders were then given by the Federal commander for the burning of the public buildings and unoccupied houses; and in a little while, to quote the language of a Federal chronicler, "the public square was surrounded by a canopy of flame; the splendid courthouse was among the buildings destroyed, with other edifices of a public character. In fact, where once stood a handsome little country town, now only remained the blackened skeletons of the houses, and the smouldering ruins that marked the track of war." In this conflagration were consumed all the principal business houses, with one accidental exception, the two brick hotels of the place, and, of course, the flames speedily spread to several dwellings occupied by women and children, and sick persons, happily rescued, however, from destruction by the exertions of the inhabitants of Oxford.

One occupied mansion, howbeit, was burned to the ground under circumstances which make the act noteworthy in these pages. It will be recollected, Mrs. Thompson's house, several days previously, had been despoiled by the Federal cavalry commander and his men. Major-General Smith now sent an officer of his staff with a detachment to burn it. Mrs. Thompson made a dignified, earnest, but vain appeal that her house might be spared her. Only fifteen minutes were granted for the removal of any articles which she might specially wish to save; but these, as fast as they were brought from the house, in the presence of Federal officers, were ruthlessly stolen from her by the soldiery who clustered around, so that scarcely an article, other than the clothing on her person, escaped fire or pillage.

Up to midday, guards had been set as if to repress pillage; these were withdrawn about that time, and for several hours thereafter Oxford was delivered up to riot and rapacity. Houses on all sides were broken into and despoiled of clothing, bedding, and provisions, which, if not carried off, were maliciously destroyed. Carpets were torn up, curtains cut down, and furniture broken in downright wantonness; and in a number of instances the torch was set to houses thus rifled, and only the exertions of their terrified occupants saved them from destruction. Some subaltern officers were greatly chagrined, and displayed a disposition to restrain their men from acts so disgraceful to their vaunted flag; but no officer of rank was heard to interpose his authority for the suppression of disorder in a place which there had been no effort to defend, nor any conflict in its immediate vicinity. The men, thus assured of the countenance of their commander, set all opposition to their licentiousness at defiance, until five P.M., when they were suddenly withdrawn, and the enemy began their retreat northward so rapidly as to reach Holly Springs by ten A.M., on the next day.

So completely, however, had they done their work in Oxford, that its non-combatant inhabitants, mostly women and children, were left absolutely destitute of food until the soldiers' rough rations could be brought up from the Confederate depots south of the Yocona [River], and distributed among them.[118]

The looting and burning of homes, along with the torturing and killing of captured prisoners of war is, of course, illegal and immoral, as is torturing and killing noncombatants and civilians. But military and religious law did not prevent Lincoln's forces from engaging in both of these monstrous practices. There was, for instance, the infamous case of Confederate Captain Sam L. Freeman, a much beloved, heavy set Christian officer who was captured at the Battle of Franklin I (April 10, 1863).[119]

Union General William T. Sherman.

As he was being marched off to prison—prodded along and beaten from all sides by his pitiless Union captors—the weary Rebel leader began to lag behind, stumbling on the path. He was then ordered to run, an impossible task, as he had once again fallen to the ground exhausted.[120] Instead of helping him to his feet and assisting him along, as required by both international military law and moral ethics, a member of the Fourth U.S. Cavalry rode up to Captain Freeman and shot him in the head at point blank range, killing him instantly.[121] His body was left unceremoniously on the dusty road where he fell.[122]

Prior to the shooting, Freeman had told the Yank who was about to murder him that he could go no faster, and never once did he resist or try to flee. When Forrest arrived on the scene his eyes were already filled with tears. He took Freeman's cold hand and said "Brave man; none braver!"[123] Forrest and his soldiers were "stricken with grief" and filled with vengeance, retaining the memory of this horrific event for the remainder of the War.[124]

Long before the Battle of Fort Pillow, Forrest's men were well aware of the Yankee approach to warfare embodied in such Union officers as Sherman, and the equally hated General Philip Henry Sheridan, who needlessly destroyed Virginia's Shenandoah Valley. According to the U.S. government's own official records, Sherman ordered the burning of homes and the killing of civilians as he lumbered through the Southland preying on the helpless and the innocent.[125] He even forced captured, unprotected Confederate soldiers to clear their own minefields, an incident that the cocky Yank joyfully recorded in his *Memoirs*:

> . . . the rebels had planted eight-inch shells in the road, with friction-matches to explode them by being trodden on. This was not war, but murder, and it made me very angry. I immediately ordered a lot of rebel prisoners to be brought from the provost-guard, armed with picks and spades, and made them march in close order along the road, so as to explode their own torpedoes, or to discover and dig them up. They begged hard, but I reiterated the order, and could hardly help laughing at their stepping so gingerly along the road, where it was supposed sunken torpedoes might explode at each step, but they found no other torpedoes till near Fort McAllister.[126]

It is known today that such illicit activities against Confederate soldiers were sanctioned by both Grant and Lincoln, which is hardly surprising since, as the *Official Records* clearly show, both were war criminals themselves.

3

UNION RENEGADES & GENERAL DISORDER

GALVANIZED YANKS, DESERTERS, & TURNCOATS

THERE WERE OTHER IMPORTANT FACTORS that influenced the outcome at Fort Pillow. One of the Union commanders at the fort, Major Bradford, along with many of his men, were "galvanized Yanks," or "homemade Yanks"; that is, Southerners who had joined Lincoln's Northern army.[127] Some of them, according to at least one account, appear to have formerly served under Forrest.[128] Bradford himself, a practicing lawyer at Dyersburg, Tennessee, was a Middle Tennessee native, the same area Forrest was from.

Adding to the problem for Forrest and his men was the fact that many of Bradford's soldiers were deserters from the Rebel army, nearly all whose families had sided with Jeff Davis and the South.[129] There were few things worse to the General than a deserter or a turncoat, particularly a Confederate one. As one who had killed deserters from his own ranks,[130] Forrest definitely would not have been pleased when he heard this news.

It is probable then, if not a dead certainty, that on April 12, 1864, he and his troops marched toward Fort Pillow with military law on their minds. For Forrest would have been very much within his rights as a Rebel officer to hunt down Confederate deserters and bring them to justice—as his own commander, General Hood, had ordered him to.[131]

But there was something else, for Forrest something worse still: the galvanized Yanks from his neighborhood had not joined the North out of any kind of nationalistic pride in the Union. They were at Fort Pillow strictly to partake in the illicit activities of the "lair" of Federal soldiers there: the harassment, molestation, robbery, burglary, mugging, pillaging, rape, and murder of loyal Southerners in the area (mostly women, children, and old men).[132] Forrest boiled at the mere thought of such treasonous deception.

This 19th-Century illustration, one of the greatest pieces of anti-South propaganda ever fabricated, is a fictitious Yankee depiction of the Battle of Fort Pillow. Here, Confederate soldiers are shown "killing Union troops after they surrendered." If this is actually what had happened, it would have been a flagrant and heinous violation of the Geneva Conventions. Forrest's officers, whose ethics were known to have been "beyond reproach," would have reported him to Confederate authorities, and he would have been arrested, tried, and imprisoned. Yet, no Confederate reports of a "crime" were ever filed and Forrest was never court-martialed. In fact, the opposite transpired. The Confederate Congress later personally thanked the General and his men "for their late brilliant and successful campaign" in West Tennessee.

Is it possible that he may have also attacked Fort Pillow, in part, out of resentment and revenge? While such behavior would not have been officially condoned at Richmond, if he did it is certainly understandable. For Forrest's men the Battle of Fort Pillow was, in some respects, more a local feud than an impersonal fight with strangers. They knew many of the enemy personally, and before the war had been neighbors, even friends. The Yankees' torture and murder of their fellow comrades in arms, along with the growing criminal activities of other Northern troops, and the knowledge of their desertion from the Southern army, no doubt weighed heavily upon their minds that Spring day as they approached the garrison.[133]

COMPLEXITIES & CONFUSION AT FORT PILLOW

There were still other factors that contributed to the disaster at the Tennessee garrison.

There was the difficult and confusing topography surrounding the fort, which itself was situated on an elevated point of land overlooking two bodies of water: the Mississippi River and Cold Creek. Adding to the complexity of the terrain were numerous bluffs, hollows, knolls, gullies, large logs and stumps, steep embankments, overhangs, dense underbrush, muddy river banks, and ravines (one that was 450 feet deep, the height of a forty-five story building).[134]

We must also mention that there were a series of unexpected events over which Forrest had no control. One example will suffice.

Midway through the conflict a segment of the Yankee troops agreed to surrender and sent up white flags of truce. Only yards away, however, other Federal troops continued to pour canister into the Confederate lines, refusing to give up the struggle.[135]

About this time, several boats, the *Olive Branch*, the *Hope*, and the *M. R. Cheek* (at least one a Yankee steamer and another a Yankee gunboat—both bristling with soldiers and artillery), chugged toward Fort Pillow's river landing.[136] Another Yankee gunboat, the *New Era*, already menacingly docked on the river just past the fort, was operating under a prearranged agreement with Yankee General Bradford that if the breastworks were taken by the Rebels, it was to offer assistance by giving shelter to escaping Union soldiers under a canopy of protective canister.[137]

The three aforementioned boats, meanwhile, continued to approach the landing, wholly ignoring the white truce flags that were fluttering in the breeze in plain sight: under the rules of military engagement the steamers should have "put about" and moved away.[138]

Emboldened by the sight of their boats plying toward the fort with promised assistance and reinforcements, those Yanks who had previously agreed to surrender decided to fight on, this time with renewed vigor. The intoxicated blacks in particular—now "indifferent to danger or death"—fought on with insane determination, egged on by the ridiculous Yankee lie that Forrest's men had taken an oath to "automatically kill all captured Negroes."[139]

Making an already terrible situation even worse, they did not realize, or did not care, that they had left the Union flags of truce flying.[140] Additionally, a signal flag should have been sent up signifying that a truce was being discussed. The Yankees at the fort, however, never hoisted this particular flag.[141]

Adding to an already disastrous situation was the fact that, after the breastworks were overrun by the Confederates, the Yankee gunboats, in particular the *New Era*, did not offer either the promised "succor" or "shower of canister" to cover the fleeing Yanks (in fact, the *New Era* later "disappeared up the river").[142] As a result, the bewildered, scrambling Union mob, many in a state of drunkenness, threw themselves into either the Mississippi River or Cold Creek and drowned.[143]

Of course, in the mass confusion that ensued on both sides, Confederate and Federal, more unnecessary injuries and deaths occurred. Had the inebriated blacks alone simply surrendered, most of this carnage would have been avoided.[144]

Confederate General James R. Chalmers.

4

THE CHARGES
AGAINST FORREST

DID FORREST KILL WOMEN & CHILDREN AT FORT PILLOW?

LET US NOW LOOK AT the main accusations hurled at Forrest, beginning with the detestable imputation that during the Confederate attack he and his men killed innocent civilians, including women and children, who were hiding inside the fort.

There were indeed male civilians in the garrison at the time, but they had voluntarily elected to stay and fight. As for women and children, however, the *Official Records* make no mention of them. The reason is that they were taken away by boat before the fighting began, as Yankees at the fort themselves testified. One of these, Union surgeon Dr. Charles Fitch, later avowed:

> Early in the morning all of the woman and all of the non-combatants were ordered on to some barges, and were towed by a gunboat up the river to an island before any one was hurt.[145]

BURIED ALIVE?

What about the charge that the Rebels buried wounded and dying Yankees alive?

Smouldering ruins were extinguished by throwing dirt on them. If a few Union men were partially buried at this time, there is a simple and innocent explanation: a number of soldiers were "dead" drunk, while others simply "played dead" to escape being captured.[146] It is entirely possible that a few individuals from each of these two categories were "buried." However, their "graves" would have been extremely shallow and they could have gotten up and walked away with little effort, hardly qualifying as being "buried alive."

As for the dead who were interred properly at the scene, the Confederates were not involved, as Federal forces were entirely responsible for burying their own. Actually, far from participating in such outrages, Forrest conscientiously allowed the surviving Yanks to reenter the fort and remove their wounded and bury their dead. The General and his men even helped carry wounded Yanks from the field, carefully and respectfully placing them in tents and barracks where they could be tended to by their own surgeons.[147]

At the Battle of Fort Pillow, Union Lieutenant Mack J. Leaming delivers the fateful reply to Forrest's men: "We will not surrender."

As proof that no Yankee was subjected to murderous or even inhumane behavior by the Rebs, we have the fact that many of the injured Federal soldiers, both white *and* black, were actually treated by Forrest's own doctors[148] under his usual humane order to give attention "to the wounded on both sides."[149] The official report of Confederate Major Charles W. Anderson, dated February 3, 1864, validates these claims:

> The general says have the salt rolled out, so that it will be safe, and then burn up all the houses at the fort except the one used as hospital. Leave the Federal surgeon and such of the wounded as cannot travel or be moved, and parole them; also parole and leave with them a nurse or two, or slightly wounded men sufficient to wait on them, sending forward all other prisoners and negroes to Jackson immediately.

No negroes will be delivered to their owners on the march; they must all go to Jackson. Leave with the wounded five or six days' supply of provisions and any medicine they may need; the balance of provisions issue to your command.[150]

BURNED ALIVE?

Another serious charge against Forrest is that *during* the battle he and his men purposefully burned wounded black Yanks alive in their tents and cabins. First, the "burning incident" occurred on April 13, the day *after* the battle. Second, no one could have been burned alive because all of the wounded had been evacuated by then. The exact series of events were as follows.

On the morning of the 13th, Forrest sent a detail back to the fort under Major Anderson to bury the "overlooked dead" and collect any remaining weapons. A Union gunboat, the *Silver Cloud*, then appeared on the scene and began to fire upon the men.[151] As there was no longer any reason to guard the fort, and as they were now under attack by a Yankee gunboat on the river, Anderson ordered his men to vacate the area.[152]

As was the military custom in these situations, upon retreat the enemy's remaining tents and cabins were set ablaze to prevent their contents from being recaptured by the Federals, who were already returning to defend what was left of the fort. The Rebs had no way of knowing this, but there were several dead black soldiers inside the structures, killed during the conflict the day before. Yanks who later came on the scene understandably misunderstood what they saw.[153] It was this action that gave rise to the patently false rumor that "Forrest had burned black soldiers alive in their tents."[154] As we will see, Forrest himself was miles away at the time.

CRUCIFIED YANKS?

Forrest's harshest critics claim that he and his men nailed Union soldiers to wooden beams and tortured them to death. In one case it was alleged that the General pinioned a Yank, Lieutenant J. C. Akerstrom, to the side of a house by his clothing and lit him on fire, burning him alive.

Yet, Union testimony itself contradicted these accusations. In the case of Akerstrom, for example, Federal Private John F. Ray later testified that the lieutenant had been killed during the battle, falling dead right in front of him.[155]

In short, this charge is so patently absurd it scarcely deserves mention. It is false for the same reasons all of the other accusations against Forrest and his men in this chapter are false.[156]

DID FORREST MURDER MAJOR BRADFORD?

Charges were later brought against Forrest for the "murder" of Yankee Major William F. Bradford based on the testimony of a Union conscript, who testified that he witnessed the shooting, and that Bradford had been on his knees "begging for his life." But is this story true?

Again Confederate fact turns out to be quite different than Northern myth.

After capture Bradford was to be paroled to "supervise the burial of his [recently deceased] brother." The night before, giving his word of honor that he would not try to escape, he was placed in a tent under light guard. That evening, however, he slipped out of the tent and into the darkness.[157] Recaptured, he was now placed under heavy guard.[158]

The next day, en route to Brownsville, Tennessee, Bradford was being guarded at the rear by five of Forrest's men. Suddenly, he bolted, trying to make another escape. In accordance to military law, he was legally and rightfully shot down, a far cry from being "gunned down in cold blood" under Forrest's order, as pro-North authors claim.[159]

Confederate Lieutenant A. H. French.

As Forrest's official report shows below, the General himself, at the front of his command at the time this occurred, did not even hear about Bradford's death until some ten days later.[160] We will further point out that there were no Confederate officers of any kind involved. This was strictly a "private" matter.[161]

Yet, if personal vengeance had been wished upon Bradford by Forrest's men, he could have easily been slain during the battle itself. Instead, he was captured and treated with "the utmost consideration and civility." It was his second escape attempt that changed his fate. At that point Forrest's men decided to shoot the war criminal rather than hang him, a difference with little distinction under the circumstances.[162]

It must also be asked, if Bradford was killed "in cold blood" by Forrest or anyone else, why is there nothing in the *Official Records* pertaining to the arrest, trial, and imprisonment of Bradford's murderers?[163] Where, in other words, is the evidence?

COMMON THIEVERY?

Finally, there is the accusation that Forrest and his men raided and robbed the fort after dark, stealing valuables from the dead and committing other serious offences on the night of April 12.

According to official reports Forrest's *entire* cavalry was well clear of the area by sunset (6:00 PM),[164] as by that time he had made camp some fifteen miles away[165] at a farmhouse to the east (on their way back to Jackson, Tennessee).[166] In fact, Forrest himself left the scene of the battle as soon as it was over that afternoon and never returned. His men soon followed, leaving no Confederates at the fort after sundown.[167]

The nighttime depredations at Fort Pillow can, no doubt, be attributed to one of the many gangs of thugs, bummers, and ne'er-do-wells that roamed the South at the time, preying on the weak and the defenseless. It was not uncommon to see one of these shameless packs of "hyenas," as Wyeth referred to them, on the smouldering battlefield after a conflict, running from body to body, rifling through the pockets of the wounded and the deceased.[168]

On March 21, 1864, just weeks before Fort Pillow, Forrest made mention of these gangs in a field report to Confederate Lieutenant Colonel Thomas M. Jack:

> The whole of West Tennessee is overrun by bands and squads of robbers, horse thieves and deserters, whose depredations and unlawful appropriations of private property are rapidly and effectually depleting the country.[169]

TRUMPED UP CHARGES & FALSE STORIES

Later, Yankee newspapers distorted, exaggerated, and even concocted various events pertaining to Fort Pillow. Why? The usual reason for 19th-Century Yankee yellow journalism: it was another attempt to justify

Lincoln's illegal invasion of the South and the Northern hatred of her citizens. Fort Pillow thus became the usual "atrocity story," bloodied up for Northern consumption.

Confederate Colonel Robert McCulloch.

Since the tale of the "massacre" was particularly distasteful to freed slaves, L i n c o l n   a n d   h i s administration naturally made the most of the trumped-up stories (inciting more discord, racism, and violence), all of which have been handed down to us today as "fact."

But the truth has risen to the surface, despite the North's ongoing attempts to suppress it: later, during the Fort Pillow tribunal, most of the affidavits attesting to Forrest's "butchery" at Fort Pillow, in fact, came from Yankee blacks who were illiterate and could not even sign their own names. As such, the resultant documents were "conflicting and extravagant."[170] Why? Who wrote out this ridiculous paperwork?

Obviously the incriminating "evidence" was illegally penciled in by South-hating Northern whites who had but one intention: to permanently disgrace Forrest and taint his name.

There is also the fact that at least 23 percent (eighteen out of seventy-eight) of those who testified against Forrest were not eyewitnesses, yet their statements were treated with the same solemnity as those who were actually at the scene. Here we have proof that the U.S. government, which revealingly called its final report on the "massacre" a "war measure," tried to create a case against Forrest out of nothing for the sole purpose of tarnishing his reputation and humiliating the South.[171] Neither Forrest or any of his subordinates ever ordered a massacre, or even anything illegal. In short, the Union report was anti-South wartime propaganda, pure and simple.[172]

5

HOW IT ALL STARTED

THE BEGINNING OF THE LIE

MUCH OF THE NEFARIOUS ANTI-FORREST mythology concerning Fort Pillow began with Yankee Adjutant Mack J. Leaming, whose official view of an important event during the battle was based on a visual error.

On the afternoon of April 12th, as the four water craft—one Yankee gunboat (the *New Era*) and three steamers (one laden with Yankee troops)—approached to reinforce the fort, Leaming believed Forrest violated the flag of truce. This occurred when the Yankee officer thought he saw Forrest move some of his men into a ravine near the river in order to shell the oncoming boats *while the truce flag was flying*. In his official report Leaming wrote of the supposed incident:

> During the cessation of firing on both sides, in consequence of the flag of truce offered by the enemy, and while the attention of both officers and men was naturally directed to the south side of the fort where the communications were being received and answered, Forrest had resorted to means the most foul and infamous ever adopted in the most barbarous ages of the world for the accomplishment of his design. Here he took occasion to move his troops, partially under cover of a ravine and thick underbrush, into the very position he had been fighting to obtain throughout the entire engagement, up to 3.30 p. m.[173]

In reality, the Confederates had not just moved into the ravine. They had captured this area much earlier in the day, long before the flag of truce had been raised. What Leaming saw were some of Forrest's troops, under Confederate Colonel C. R. Barteau, moving *out of the ravine they had already occupied* in order to stop the Yankee boats loaded with artillery and infantry from coming ashore. As the Yankees had not signaled their boats to stop and turn around (as they should have done under military regulations regarding truces), Forrest had every right to do whatever was necessary to prevent them from landing.[174]

Confederate Major
Charles W. Anderson.

Forrest himself vehemently denied Leaming's accusation, as did his other officers, Chalmers, Bell, McCulloch, and Anderson, among many others. What is more, even Yankee officers corroborated Forrest's side of the story. One of these, Union General George F. Shepley, who had been aboard one of the boats (the *Olive Branch*) driving toward the fort, fully backed Forrest and his officers in his report to the U.S. Committee on the Conduct of the War.[175]

As this document completely exonerates Forrest, it is worth including here.

Report of Brig. Gen. George F. Shepley, U. S. Army, of Affairs, April 12.
HEADQUARTERS NORFOLK AND PORTSMOUTH
Norfolk, VA May 7, 1864.
SIR: At my own request, having been relieved from duty as military governor of Louisiana and ordered to report for duty to the commanding general of the army, I left New Orleans on the evening of the 6th of April as a passenger in the *Olive Branch*, New Orleans and Saint Louis passenger steamer, not in the service of the Government, but loaded with male and female passengers and cargo of private parties. The steamer was unarmed, and had no troops and no muskets for protection against guerrillas when landing at woodyards and other places.

The boat stopped at Vicksburg, and I went ashore. When I returned to the boat, as she was about leaving, I found that a detachment of a portion of the men of two batteries—one Ohio and one Missouri—belonging to the Seventeenth Army Corps, with the horses, guns, caissons, wagons, tents, and baggage of the two batteries, had been put on board, with orders, as I afterward learned on inquiring, to report to General Brayman at Cairo.

The horses occupied all of the available space, fore and aft, on the sides of the boilers and machinery, which were on deck. The guns, caissons, baggage wagons, tents, garrison and camp equipage were piled up together on the bows, leaving only space for the gang-plank.

The men had no small-arms, so that when the boat landed, as happened in one instance, at a wood-yard where guerrillas had just passed, the pickets thrown out to prevent surprise were necessarily unarmed.

As the boat was approaching, and before it was in sight of Fort Pillow, some females hailed it from the shore, and said the rebels had attacked Fort Pillow and captured two boats on the river, and would take us if we went on.

The captain of the *Olive Branch* said they had probably taken the *Mollie Abel*, which was due there about that time from Saint Louis. He turned his boat, saying he would go back to Memphis.

I objected to going back; stopped the boat below the next point hailed another smaller steamer without passengers, which I saw approaching, and ordered it alongside. I ordered the captain of this boat to cast off the coal barges he had in tow, and take me on board with a section of a battery to go to Fort Pillow. While he was trying to disencumber his boat of the coal barges, another boat, better fitted for the purpose (the [*M. R.*] *Cheek*), hove in sight. Finding that I could get her ready quicker than the other, I had her brought alongside and went aboard myself with Captain Thornton, of my staff, and Captain Williams, the ranking officer of the batteries. Before we could get the guns on board, a steamer with troops hove in sight coining down the river from Fort Pillow. We could not distinguish at first whether they were Union or rebel soldiers.

I asked Captain Pegram, of the *Olive Branch*, if the story of the women turned out to be true and the rebels had the steamer, could his boat sink her. Captain Pegram replied: "Yes, my boat can run right over her." I ordered him to swing out into the stream to be ready for her. When she approached we saw U.S. infantry soldiers on board that had just passed the fort. She kept on going rapidly down with the current, only hailing the *Olive Branch*: "All right up there; you can go by. The gun-boat is lying off the fort." This steamer was the *Liberty*.

We then proceeded up the river in the *Olive Branch*. Near Fort Pillow some stragglers or guerrillas fired from the shore with musketry, aiming at the pilot-house.

I was then in the pilot-house, and, as we kept on, I

observed that one of the two other boats I have mentioned, which followed us at some distance, was compelled to put back. The *Olive Branch* kept on to report to the gun-boat on the station.

An officer came off from the gun-boat in a small boat, and said he did not want any boat to stop; ordered us to go on to Cairo, and tell captain (name not recollected) to send him immediately 400 rounds of ammunition. There was no firing at the fort at this time. The Union flag was flying, and after we had passed the fort we could see a "flag of truce" outside the fortifications.

No signal of any kind was made to the boat from the fort or from the shore.

No intimation was given us from the gun-boat, which had the right to order a steamer of this description, other than the order to proceed to Cairo to send down the ammunition.

From the fact that the *Liberty* had just passed down the river from the fort, with troops on board; from her hailing us to go by, and continuing her course down the river without stopping; that no signal was made the *Olive Branch* from the fort on the shore, and no attack was being made on the fort at the time; that the officer of the gun-boat said he did not want any boats to stop, and ordered the captain of the *Olive Branch* to go on and have ammunition sent down to him by first boat, I considered, and now consider, that the captain of the *Olive Branch* was not only justified in going on, but bound to proceed. The *Olive Branch* was incapable of rendering any assistance, being entirely defenseless. If any guns could have been placed in position on the boat, they could not have been elevated to reach sharpshooters on the high, steep bluff outside the fort. A very few sharpshooters from the shore near the fort could have prevented any landing, and have taken the boat. We supposed the object of the rebels was rather to seize a boat to effect a crossing into Arkansas than to capture the fort. We had no means of knowing or suspecting that so strong a position as Fort Pillow had not been properly garrisoned for defense, when it was in constant communication with General Hurlbut at Memphis.

The *Olive Branch* had just left Memphis, General Hurlbut's headquarters, where it had been during the previous night. If it had not been for the appearance of the *Liberty*, I should have attempted a landing at Fort Pillow in the small steamer. If any intimation had been given from the gun-boat, or the shore, I should have landed personally from the *Olive Branch*. The order given to the contrary prevented it.

Coming from New Orleans, and having no knowledge of affairs in that military district, I could not presume that a fort, with uninterrupted water communication above and below, could possibly be without a garrison strong enough to hold it for a few hours.

. . . Captain Thornton, Twelfth Maine Volunteers, a gallant officer, distinguished for his bravery at Ponchatoula, where he was wounded and left in the hands of the enemy, was on board the *Olive Branch*, and will take this communication to the committee. I respectfully ask that he may be thoroughly examined as to all the circumstances. I am conscious that a full examination will show that I rather exceeded than neglected my duty.

I have the honor to be, with great respect, your obedient servant,

G. F. SHEPLEY, Brigadier-General, Commanding.

Hon. D. W. Good, of Committee on Conduct of the War.[176]

HOW FORREST HIMSELF CONTRIBUTED TO THE "FORT PILLOW MASSACRE" MYTH

On April 15, 1864, just three days after the fall of Fort Pillow, Forrest sent a short report concerning the battle to Confederate Lieutenant Colonel Thomas M. Jack. It was part fact, part brag. It read:

Arrived there on the morning of the 12th and attacked the place with a portion of McCulloch's and Bell's brigades, numbering about 1,500 men, and after a sharp contest captured the garrison and all of its stores. A demand was made for the surrender, which was refused. The victory was complete, and the loss of the enemy will never be known from the fact that large numbers ran into the river and were shot and drowned. The force was composed of about 500 negroes and 200 white soldiers (Tennessee Tories). The river was dyed with the blood of the slaughtered for 200 yards. There was in the fort a large number of citizens who had fled there to escape the conscript law. Most of these ran into the river and were drowned. The approximate loss was upward of 500 killed, but few of the officers escaping.[177]

We will recall that Forrest had left the scene of the battle as soon as the Confederate flag was raised above the fort. At the time accurate statistics were not yet available as to how many Yanks had been taken prisoner, how many had been wounded, how many had escaped, or how many had been killed.

As discussed earlier, it was later determined that only 231 of the 557 Yankee soldiers, 40 percent, were killed.[178] Thus Forrest's assumption, that he and his men had killed nearly 72 percent (i.e., 500 out of 700) of the Union soldiers, was wildly incorrect and greatly overstated.[179] In this unfortunate manner Forrest himself added fuel to the Northern myth that he had committed heinous war crimes at Fort Pillow.

General Nathan Bedford Forrest.

Forrest's unlucky exaggeration was indeed later used against him by none other than Yankee General Ulysses S. Grant, who, in his *Memoirs*, gleefully repeated Forrest's sentence about the river being "dyed with the blood of the slaughtered."[180] As the official numbers of the dead were available to Grant at the time he wrote this piece of Northern propaganda (1885), it is obvious that he was intentionally trying to sully Forrest's character.[181] (This is the same man who Americans, largely Northerners, later voted in as their eighteenth president, and whose face they placed on the U.S. fifty-dollar bill.)

Yet Grant's ploy worked. Thanks to this single sentence in his *Memoirs*, entirely based on Forrest's own faulty statement, the belief that a "massacre" took place at Fort Pillow has gone down in history, Yankee history at least, as objective truth. Not only is the Battle of Fort Pillow now routinely referred to as the "Fort Pillow Massacre," a number of extremely venomous, defamatory, anti-Forrest books have been published on this topic as well, further keeping the falsehood alive.[182]

(Let us note here at least one reason why such works are impossible to take seriously: most base their conclusions partly or wholly on the outrageous, farcical, unscientific, highly biased, error-ridden publication, *Fort Pillow Massacre*, printed in the Spring of 1864 by a South-hating U.S. government. Since this work was long ago discredited by Southern historians and scholars, modern anti-Forrest works based on it must also be called into question, if not rejected altogether.)

It did not help matters that Forrest's own official report of the battle got delayed in transit and was not available for public scrutiny until four months afterward.[183] This 120-day period helped allow ridiculous and damaging innuendo to grow into rumors, rumors into myth, myth into legend, and legend into "fact."

6

LINCOLN, GRANT, & SHERMAN TAKE ON FORREST

YANKS PROMISE REVENGE BUT NEVER FOLLOW THROUGH

IN WASHINGTON, D.C., WHEN LINCOLN heard about Forrest's "massacre," he immediately sent word to his Secretary of War, Edwin M. Stanton, to investigate "the alleged butchery of our troops." Stanton then contacted Grant in the field,[184] passing on Lincoln's edict, which ordered physical reprisal against Forrest and his offending officers—if found guilty.[185]

Grant bitterly denounced the affair,[186] writing furiously to Sherman on April 15:

> CULPEPER, VA.,
> April 15, 1864—8 p. m.
> Major-General SHERMAN:
> Forrest must be driven out, but with a proper commander in West Tennessee there is force enough now. Your preparations for the coming campaign must go on, but if it is necessary to detach a portion of the troops intended for it, detach them and make your campaign with that much fewer men.
>
> Relieve Maj. Gen. S. A. Hurlbut. I can send General Washburn, a sober and energetic officer, to take his place. I can also send you General L. C. Hunt to command District of Columbus. Shall I send Washburn? Does General Hurlbut think if he moves a part of his force after the only enemy within 200 miles of him that the post will run off with the balance of his force?
>
> If our men have been murdered after capture, retaliation must be resorted to promptly.

U. S. GRANT, Lieutenant-General.[187]

Grant's last sentence clearly illustrates that at the time not even the highest ranking Yankee officers believed that a massacre had taken place, or that Forrest was capable of such an act.[188]

Most revealingly of this fact, however, is that no retaliation against Forrest ever followed, not by Lincoln, Stanton, Grant, or Sherman, or anyone else for that matter.[189] And, as they had all well demonstrated throughout the War, these were not men to shrink from exacting retribution on those they deemed worthy.[190]

Union President Abraham Lincoln.

While in the South, Lincoln's refusal to avenge Fort Pillow was rightly seen as a further sign of Forrest's innocence, in the North it was taken as just another indication of the president's white supremacist sentiments.[191] Yet years later, in his memoirs, Sherman sided with Forrest, theorizing (correctly) that Forrest would never have led such a murderous assault as the alleged "massacre" ascribed to him, and was instead no doubt out of both eyesight and earshot at the rear. Wrote Sherman:

> . . . I am told that Forrest personally disclaims any active participation in the assault, and that he stopped the firing as soon as he could. I also take it for granted that Forrest did not lead the assault in person, and consequently that he was to the rear, out of sight if not of hearing at the time, and I was told by hundreds of our men, who were at various times prisoners in Forrest's possession, that he was usually very kind to them.[192]

Indeed, it was the testimony of both Confederate and Union eyewitnesses on the stand before the U.S. government's investigative committee that later proved Forrest's innocence.[193] One from the latter category, Union Dr. Charles Fitch, said that he had always believed that

Forrest never knew anything about any kind of "massacre."[194]

Another Yankee, the aforementioned Adjutant Mack J. Leaming, agreed, testifying under oath that Forrest was nowhere in sight during the height of the alleged "massacre," and that when the General heard about uncontrolled Rebel shooting he immediately ordered a cease-fire:

> U.S. Government Committee: Did you observe any effort on the part of their [Confederate] officers to suppress the murders?
> Leaming: No, sir; I did not see any [murders] where I was first carried; just about dusk, all at once several shots were fired just outside. The cry was: "They are shooting the darkey soldiers." I heard an officer ride up and say: "Stop that firing; arrest that man." I suppose it was a rebel officer, but I do not know. It was reported to me, at the time, that several darkeys were shot then. An officer who stood by me, a prisoner, said that they had been shooting them, but that the general [Forrest] had had it stopped.[195]

Yet another Union officer at Fort Pillow, Captain John G. Woodruff, testified that any Negroes killed at the battle "were not killed by General Forrest's orders." Rather, Forrest "stopped the massacre as soon as he was able to do so."[196] More to the point, Confederate clergyman, David C. Kelley,

> now a minister at Columbia, Tennessee, testifies that a day or two after the fight at Fort Pillow, in a conversation with General Forrest in regard to the colored troops, the general said that he was opposed to the killing of negro troops; that it was his policy to capture all he could and return them to their owners.[197]

Despite the obvious jaundiced perspective in Fitch's, Woodruff's, and Leaming's statements, they and many others like them left the U.S. government little choice when it came to Forrest's involvement: subsequently he was cleared of all charges of wrongdoing in connection with Fort Pillow, a decree that the modern anti-Forrest movement still refuses to accept.[198] Not even the pronouncement of the *Encyclopedia Britannica* could ever change their minds. According to the that venerable work, "it seems probable that Forrest himself . . . whose military character was admittedly that of a great leader . . . had no part in [the alleged massacre]."[199]

The Confederates invading Fort Pillow, April 12, 1864.

7

THE EVIDENCE:
OFFICIAL REPORTS

TESTIMONY OF FORREST'S AID-DE-CAMP, MAJOR CHARLES W. ANDERSON

THIRTY-FOUR YEARS AFTER FORT Pillow, one of Forrest's officers, Major Charles W. Anderson, who was at the battle with his commander, gave the following sworn affidavit before W. H. Hindman, the Notary Public of Rutherford County, Tennessee, on February 23, 1898:

> I, Charles W. Anderson, of Florence, Rutherford County and State of Tennessee, do solemnly swear that I was at the time Captain of Cavalry and Acting Adjutant-General on the staff of General N. B. Forrest, and was the only member of the staff with him at the capture of Fort Pillow, April 12, 1864. Before the assault on the works I was temporarily placed in command of three companies of dismounted men from McCulloch's brigade, and ordered to take position on the face of the bluff just below the fort, and prevent the landing of steamers (then approaching) during truce.
>
> When Forrest's last and imperative demand for immediate surrender was refused, the general in person ordered me to "hold my position on the bluff, prevent any escape of the garrison by water, to pour rifle-balls into the open ports of the *New Era* when she went into action, and to fight everything blue betwixt wind and water until yonder flag comes down."
>
> When driven from the works, the garrison retreated towards the river, with guns in hand, and firing back, and as soon as in view we opened fire on them, and continued it rapidly until

the Federal flag came down, when firing was stopped at once, the detachment ordered back to their regiment, and in less than two minutes after the flag came down I joined the general inside of the works.

To the best of my knowledge and belief it did not exceed twenty minutes from the time our bugles sounded for the assault until the fort was in our possession and firing had ceased on every part of the ground.

I further swear that six cases of rifle ammunition were found on the face of the bluff, in the immediate rear of the fort, with tops removed and ready for immediate distribution and use; also that about two hundred and seventy-five serviceable rifles and carbines were gathered up between the water's edge and the brow of the bluff, where they had been thrown down by the garrison when they found the gunboat *New Era* had deserted them and escape impossible. As my command did the most destructive as well as the very last firing done at Fort Pillow, the testimony of certain witnesses made before a sub-committee of the United States Congress, that a massacre of the garrison took place after capture, is false, and I further swear that to the best of my knowledge and belief the heavy loss in killed and wounded during their retreat was alone due to the incapacity of their commander, the drunken condition of the men, and the fatal agreement with and promise of Captain Marshall of the *New Era* to protect and succor them when driven from the works.

Charles W. Anderson. State of Tennessee, County of Rutherford, February 23, 1898.[200]

CONFEDERATE REALITY

The truth about Fort Pillow is that Forrest himself never participated in any of the claimed atrocities. For one thing, he was not present at the front line (when and where these events were supposed to have taken place), and when he did reach it, he ordered his troops to pull back and cease fire. Also, in the midst of battle, when one of his horses was shot out from under him, it fell on Forrest, disabling him for several days after.[201]

Obviously blameless, at the close of

Confederate Brigadier-General Tyree H. Bell.

the War, both Federal eyewitnesses and the U.S. government cleared Forrest of all charges.[202] Despite this, the Fort Pillow debacle and indictments of racism have been affixed to Forrest for fifteen decades.

In reality, Forrest was no respecter of race. He captured or killed all Yanks, whatever their skin color, with the same swift and unerring force. As we will see, he himself said:

> . . . I slaughter no man except in open warfare, and . . . my prisoners, both white and black, are turned over to my Government to be dealt with as it may direct.[203]

Indeed, while forty-five of his own black servants fought in his integrated command at the Battle of Fort Pillow, the white and black Yankee soldiers inside the garrison were segregated—per Lincoln's orders.[204]

Forrest was not a racist. He was a Yankeeist.

FORREST'S OFFICIAL FORT PILLOW REPORT
What follows is General Forrest's full official field report of the Battle of Fort Pillow.

> HEADQUARTERS FORREST'S CAVALRY DEPARTMENT, Jackson, Tenn., April 26, 1864.
> COLONEL: I have the honor respectfully to forward you the following report of my engagement with the enemy on the 12th instant at Fort Pillow:
> My command consisted of McCulloch's brigade, of Chalmers' division, and Bell's brigade, of Buford's division, both placed for the expedition under the command of Brig. Gen. James R. Chalmers, who, by a forced march, drove in the enemy's pickets, gained possession of the outer works, and by the time I reached the field, at 10 a. m., had forced the enemy to their main fortifications, situated on the bluff or bank of the Mississippi River at the mouth of Cold Creek. The fort is an earth-work, crescent shaped, is 8 feet in height and 4 feet across the top, surrounded by a ditch 6 feet deep and 12 feet in width, walls sloping to the ditch but perpendicular inside. It was garrisoned by 700 troops with six pieces of field artillery. A deep ravine surrounds the fort, and from the fort to the ravine the ground descends rapidly. Assuming command, I ordered General Chalmers to advance his lines and gain position on the slope, where our men would be perfectly protected from the heavy fire of artillery and musketry, as the

enemy could not depress their pieces so as to rake the slopes, nor could they fire on them with small-arms except by mounting the breast-works and exposing themselves to the fire of our sharpshooters, who, under cover of stumps and logs, forced them to keep down inside the works. After several hours hard fighting the desired position was gained, not, however, without considerable loss. Our main line was now within an average distance of 100 yards from the fort, and extended from Cold Creek, on the right, to the bluff, or bank, of the Mississippi River on the left.

During the entire morning the gun-boat kept up a continued fire in all directions, but without effect, and being confident of my ability to take the fort by assault, and desiring to prevent further loss of life, I sent, under flag of truce, a demand for the unconditional surrender of the garrison, a copy of which demand is hereto appended, marked No. 1, to which I received a reply, marked No. 2. The gun-boat had ceased firing, but the smoke of three other boats ascending the river was in view, the foremost boat apparently crowded with troops, and believing the request for an hour was to gain time for re-enforcements to arrive, and that the desire to consult the officers of the gun-boat was a pretext by which they desired improperly to communicate with her, I at once sent this reply, copy of which is numbered 3, directing Captain [W. A.] Goodman, assistant adjutant-general of Brigadier-General Chalmers, who bore the flag, to remain until he received a reply or until the expiration of the time proposed.

My dispositions had all been made, and my forces were in a position that would enable me to take the fort with less loss than to have withdrawn under fire, and it seemed to me so perfectly apparent to the garrison that such was the case, that I deemed their [capture] without further bloodshed a certainty. After some little delay, seeing a message delivered to Captain Goodman, I rode up myself to where the notes were received and delivered. The answer was handed me, written in pencil on a slip of paper, without envelope, and was, as well as I remember, in these words: "Negotiations will not attain the desired object." As the officers who were in charge of the Federal flag of truce had expressed a doubt as to my presence, and had pronounced the demand a trick, I handed them back the note saying: "I am General Forrest; go back and say to Major Booth that I demand an answer in plain, unmistakable English. Will he fight or surrender?" Returning to my original position, before the expiration of twenty minutes I received a reply, copy of which is marked No. 4.

While these negotiations were pending the steamers from below were rapidly approaching the fort. The foremost was the

Olive Branch, whose position and movements indicated her intention to land. A few shots fired into her caused her to leave the shore and make for the opposite. One other boat passed up on the far side of the river, the third one turned back.

Confederate soldiers "picking off the Federals at Fort Pillow."

The time having expired, I directed Brigadier-General Chalmers to prepare for the assault. Bell's brigade occupied the right, with his extreme right resting on Coal [Cold] Creek. McCulloch's brigade occupied the left, extending from the center to the river. Three companies of his left regiment were placed in an old rifle-pit on the left and almost in the rear of the fort, which had evidently been thrown up for the protection of sharpshooters or riflemen in supporting the water batteries below. On the right a portion of Barteau's regiment, of Bell's brigade, was also under the bluff and in rear of the fort. I dispatched staff officers to Colonels Bell and McCulloch, commanding brigades, to say to them that I should watch with interest the conduct of the troops; that Missourians, Mississippians, and Tennesseans surrounded the works, and I desired to see who would first scale the fort. Fearing the gun-boats and transports might attempt a landing, I directed my aide-de-camp, Capt. Charles W. Anderson, to assume command of the three companies on the left and rear of the fort and hold the position against anything that might come by land or water, but to take no part in the assault on the fort. Everything being ready, the bugle sounded the charge, which was made with a yell, and the works carried without a perceptible halt in any part of the line. As our troops mounted and poured into the fortification the enemy retreated toward the river, arms in hand and firing back, and their colors flying, no doubt expecting the gun-boat to shell us away from the bluff and protect them until they could be taken off or re-enforced. As they descended the bank an enfilading and deadly fire was poured into them by the troops under Captain Anderson, on the left, and Barteau's detachment on the right. Until this fire was opened upon them, at a distance varying from 30 to 100 yards, they were evidently ignorant of any force having gained their rear. The regiments which had stormed and carried the fort also poured a destructive fire into the rear of the retreating and now panic-stricken and almost decimated garrison. Fortunately for those of the enemy who survived this short but desperate struggle, some of our men cut the halyards, and the United States flag, floating from a tall mast in the center of the fort, came down. The forces stationed in the rear of the fort could see the flag, but were too far under the bluff to see the fort, and when the flag descended they ceased firing. But for this, so near were they to the enemy that few, if any, would have survived unhurt another volley. As it was, many rushed into the river and were drowned, and the actual loss of life will perhaps never be known, as there were quite a number of refugee citizens in the fort, many of whom were drowned and several killed in the retreat from the fort. In less than twenty minutes from the time the bugles sounded the charge, firing had ceased, and the work was done. One of the Parrott guns was turned on the gun-boat. She steamed off without replying. She had, as I afterward understood, expended all her ammunition, and was therefore powerless in affording the Federal garrison the aid and protection they doubtless expected of her when they retreated toward the river. Details were made, consisting of the captured Federals and negroes, in charge of their own officers, to collect together and bury the dead, which work continued until dark.

I also directed Captain Anderson to procure a skiff and take with him Captain Young, a captured Federal officer, and deliver to Captain Marshall, of the gun-boat, the message, copy of which is appended and numbered 5. All the boats and skiffs having been taken off by citizens escaping from the fort during the engagement, the message could not be delivered, although every effort was made to induce Captain Marshall to send his boat ashore by raising a white flag, with which Captain Young walked up and down the river in vain signaling her to come in or send out a boat. She finally moved off and disappeared around the bend above the fort. General Chalmers withdrew his forces from the fort before dark and encamped a few miles east of it.

On the morning of the 13th, I again dispatched Captain Anderson to Fort Pillow for the purpose of placing, if possible, the Federal wounded on board their transports, and report to me on his return the condition of affairs at the river. I respectfully refer you to his report, numbered 6.

My loss in the engagement was 20 killed and 60 wounded. That of the enemy unknown. Two hundred and twenty-eight were buried on the evening of the battle, and quite a number were buried the next day by details from the gun-boat fleet.

We captured 6 pieces of artillery, viz., two 10-pounder Parrott guns, two 12-pounder howitzers, and two brass 6-pounder guns, and about 350 stand of small-arms. The balance of the small-arms had been thrown in the river. All the small-arms were picked up where the enemy fell or threw them down. A few were in the fort, the balance scattered from the top of the hill to the water's edge.

We captured 164 Federals, 75 negro troops, and about 40 negro women and children, and after removing everything of value as far as able to do so, the warehouses, tents, &c., were destroyed by fire.

Among our severely wounded is Lieut. Col. Wiley M. Reed, assigned temporarily to the command of the Fifth Mississippi Regiment, who fell severely wounded while leading his regiment. When carried from the field he was supposed to be mortally wounded, but hopes are entertained of his ultimate recovery. He is a brave and gallant officer, a courteous gentleman, and a consistent Christian minister.

I cannot compliment too highly the conduct of Colonels Bell and McCulloch and the officers and men of their brigades, which composed the forces of Brigadier-General Chalmers. They fought with courage and intrepidity, and, without bayonets, assaulted and carried one of the strongest fortifications in the country.

On the 15th, at Brownsville, I received orders which rendered it necessary to send General Chalmers, in command of his own division and Bell's brigade, southward; hence I have no official report from him, but will, as soon as it can be obtained, forward a complete list of our killed and wounded, which has been ordered made out and forwarded at the earliest possible moment.

In closing my report I desire to acknowledge the prompt and energetic action of Brigadier-General Chalmers, commanding the forces around Fort Pillow. His faithful execution of all movements necessary to the successful accomplishment of the object of the expedition entitles him to special mention. He has reason to be proud of the conduct of the officers and men of his command for their gallantry and courage in assaulting and carrying the enemy's work without the assistance of artillery or bayonets.

To my staff, as heretofore, my acknowledgments are due for their prompt and faithful delivery of all orders.

I am, colonel, very respectfully, your obedient servant,

N. B. FORREST, Major-General, Commanding.

[Lieut. Col. THOMAS M. JACK, Assistant Adjutant- General.][205]

THE FORT PILLOW PAPERS OF GEN. LEONIDAS POLK

[First indorsement.]

AUGUST 1, 1864.

Respectfully referred to General Cooper, Adjutant and Inspector General.

These papers were found among papers of Lieutenant-General Polk and forwarded by his aide, Lieutenant Gale.

By order of President: WM. PRESTON JOHNSTON, Colonel and Aide-de-Camp.

Confederate President Jefferson Davis referred to the Yankees' version of the Battle of Fort Pillow as "slander," correctly asserting that Forrest "exhibited forbearance and clemency far exceeding the usage of war under like circumstances."

SEDDON'S OFFICIAL LETTER TO PRES. JEFFERSON DAVIS

James A. Seddon was a Confederate secretary of war under President Jefferson Davis, to whom this letter is addressed:

[Second indorsement.]

AUGUST 7, 1864.

Respectfully submitted to the President, who will not be surprised to see the groundlessness of the misrepresentations so industriously circulated by our unscrupulous enemies respecting the merciless conduct of our troops on that occasion.

J. A. SEDDON, Secretary.[207]

PRES. DAVIS' REPLY TO SEDDON

In his reply to Seddon, President Davis praises Forrest for his behavior at Fort Pillow:

[Third indorsement.]

AUGUST 10, 1864.

SECRETARY OF WAR:

It would be well to have the report and accompanying papers published in refutation of the slanders which have been promulgated by the Government of the enemy in relation to the conduct of our gallant and humane soldiers. Instead of cruelty, General Forrest, it appears, exhibited forbearance and clemency far exceeding the usage of war under like circumstances.

JEFF'N DAVIS. [President of the Confederate States of America][208]

FORREST'S OFFICIAL LETTER (1) TO CONFEDERATE GEN. STEPHEN DILL LEE

General Stephen D. Lee, who served with Forrest, was a relative of General Robert E. Lee. What follows is a letter Forrest sent to S. D. Lee pertaining to Fort Pillow:

ADDENDA.

HEADQUARTERS FORREST'S CAVALRY,

Tupelo, Miss., May 16, 1864.

Maj. Gen. S. D. LEE,

Demopolis, Ala.:

GENERAL: So much has been said by the Northern press in regard to the engagement at Fort Pillow that, at the suggestion of Colonel Brent and others, I have sent Judge Scruggs down for the purpose of conversing with, and procuring the statements of,

Captain Young and other Federal officers in regard to the matter. They are survivors of the so-called massacre, and Captain Young, who received and delivered the correspondence relative to the demand for surrender, was also with my aide-de-camp, Captain Anderson, with flag of truce on the day succeeding the capture in delivering the wounded on board the U. S. vessels. I respectfully suggest, therefore, that you furnish Judge Scruggs with such papers as will enable him to make the examination desired, as it may prove important; and inasmuch as the investigating committee appointed by the Federal President [Lincoln] have reported, a communication to Confederate authority may be made on the subject, and it is due to my command to place at the command of the War Department all the facts in the premises.

I am, general, very respectfully &c., your obedient servant,
N. B. FORREST, Major-General.[209]

FORREST'S OFFICIAL LETTER (2) TO GEN. STEPHEN DILL LEE
Another letter Forrest sent to S. D. Lee concerning Fort Pillow:

HEADQUARTERS FORREST'S CAVALRY,
Tupelo, June 24, 1864.
Maj. Gen. S. D. LEE,
Commanding Department, Meridian:

GENERAL: I have the honor herewith to inclose you copy of letter addressed to Major-General Washburn; also his letter addressed to you or the commanding officer Confederate forces near Tupelo. I have not in anywise compromised you, and leave the answer to General Washburn to yourself, provided you deem it necessary or advisable to communicate with him further. I deemed it due myself and command to say what I have said to him, but did not think it proper to make any communication over your signature.

I also have the honor to inclose you statements of Captain Young, who was captured at Fort Pillow, and you can make such use of them as you may deem necessary. As my official reports are in the hands of the Department at Richmond I did not, nor do I, consider that I have any defense to make, or attempt any refutations of the charges made by General Washburn. The character and tenor of his letter is also so outrageously insulting that but for its importance to my men—not myself—I should not have replied to it at all.

I shall forward you tomorrow a statement of the capture of Fort Pillow, by giving you a copy of communication asked for unofficially by Colonel Brent, assistant adjutant-general, and made by my aide-de-camp, Capt. C. W. Anderson.

I have taken pains, also, in my official report made to Lieutenant-General Polk, to place all the facts in the possession of the Government in order that they might meet any demands made by Federal authority.

Should you, however, think proper to place in the hands of General Washburn the papers sent you upon this subject, you are, of course, at liberty to use them. As for myself, entirely conscious of right, I have no explanations, apologies, or disavowals to make to General Washburn nor to any one else but my Government, through my superior officers.

I am, general, very respectfully, your most obedient servant,
N. B. FORREST, Major-General.[210]

OFFICIAL LETTER TO FORREST FROM CONFEDERATE GEN. LEONIDAS POLK

General Polk, a cousin of U.S. President James Knox Polk, sent Forrest a letter regarding his West Tennessee campaign, which included Fort Pillow:

> DEMOPOLIS, April 24, 1864.
> Major-General FORREST,
> Via Tupelo:
> Your brilliant campaign in West Tennessee has given me great satisfaction, and entitles you to the thanks of your countrymen. Appropriate orders in writing will be transmitted you immediately. A movement of the enemy up the Yazoo [River] has made it necessary that a division of your troops should move to meet it. I have ordered the brigade with General Chalmers and another from Okolona to move promptly so as to unite and give to General [John] Adams the support he needs. I have also ordered Morton's battery to join them.
> L. POLK, Lieutenant-General.[211]

THE CONFEDERATE CONGRESS THANKS FORREST

The Rebel Congress, like General Polk and every other true Confederate, was more than pleased with Forrest's actions at Fort Pillow. In gratitude Congress gave Forrest an official thank you:

> JOINT RESOLUTION of thanks to Maj. Gen. N. B. Forrest and the officers and men of his command, for their campaign in Mississippi, West Tennessee, and Kentucky.

Resolved by the Congress of the Confederate States of America, That the thanks of Congress are eminently due, and are hereby cordially tendered, to Maj. Gen. N. B. Forrest, and the officers and men of his command, for their late brilliant and successful campaign in Mississippi, West Tennessee, and Kentucky—a campaign which has conferred upon its authors fame as enduring as the records of the struggle which they have so brilliantly illustrated. — Approved, May 23, 1864.[212]

Fort Pillow (upper right) and the water battery as it looked in the Spring of 1864 from the Mississippi River.

FORREST RESPONDS TO AN ILL-NATURED YANK

Despite the obvious truth, the General received many unkind, biased, and threatening letters from Yankee officers after Fort Pillow. As mentioned above by Forrest in one of his reports, some of the more acerbic missives came from Union General Cadwallader C. Washburn (later to become one of the organizers of the food production company now known as General Mills).[213]

Forrest's replies to Washburn follow. In them he forcefully describes, and clears up, many of the mysteries surrounding the conflict at the Tennessee garrison:

HEADQUARTERS FORREST'S CAVALRY,
Tupelo, June 25 [23], 1864.
Maj. Gen. C. C. WASHBURN,

Commanding U. S. Forces, Memphis:
GENERAL: I have the honor to acknowledge the receipt (per flag of truce) of your letter of 17th instant, addressed to Maj. Gen. S. D. Lee, or officer commanding Confederate forces near Tupelo. I have forwarded it to General Lee with a copy of this letter.

I regard your letter as discourteous to the commanding officer of this department, and grossly insulting to myself. You seek by implied threats to intimidate him, and assume the privilege of denouncing me as a murderer and as guilty of the wholesale slaughter of the garrison at Fort Pillow, and found your assertions upon the *ex parte* testimony of your friends, the enemies of myself and country.

I shall not enter into the discussion, therefore, of any of the questions involved nor undertake any refutation of the charges made by you against myself; nevertheless, as a matter of personal privilege alone, I unhesitatingly say that they are unfounded and unwarranted by the facts. But whether these charges are true or false, they, with the question you ask as to whether negro troops when captured will be recognized and treated as prisoners of war, subject to exchange, &c., are matters which the Government of the United States and Confederate States are to decide and adjust, not their subordinate officers.

I regard captured negroes as I do other captured property and not as captured soldiers, but as to how regarded by my Government and the disposition which has been and will hereafter be made of them, I respectfully refer you through the proper channel to the authorities at Richmond. It is not the policy nor the interest of the South to destroy the negro—on the contrary, to preserve and protect him—and all who have surrendered to us have received kind and humane treatment.

Since the war began I have captured many thousand Federal prisoners, and they, including the survivors of the Fort Pillow massacre (black and white), are living witnesses of the fact that with my knowledge or consent, or by my order, not one of them has ever been insulted or in any way maltreated.

You speak of your forbearance in not giving to your negro troops instructions and orders as to the course they should pursue in regard to Confederate soldiers that might fall into their (your) hands, which clearly conveys to my mind two very distinct impressions. The first is that in not giving them instructions and orders you have left the matter entirely to the discretion of the negroes as to how they should dispose of prisoners; second, an implied threat to give such orders as will lead to "consequences too fearful for contemplation." In confirmation of the correctness of the first impression (which your language now fully develops), I refer you most respectfully to my letter from the battle-field of Tishomingo Creek and forwarded you by flag of truce on the 14th instant. As to the second impression, you seem disposed to take into your own hands the settlements which belong to, and can only be settled by, your Government, but if you are prepared to take upon yourself the responsibility of inaugurating a system of warfare contrary to civilized usages, the onus as well as the consequences will be chargeable to yourself.

Deprecating, as I should do, such a state of affairs, determined as I am not to be instrumental in bringing it about, feeling and knowing as I do that I have the approval of my Government, my people, and my own conscience, as to the past, and with the firm belief that I will be sustained by them in my future policy, it is left with you to determine what that policy shall be—whether in accordance with the laws of civilized nations or in violation of them.

I am, general, yours, very respectfully,
N. B. FORREST, Major- General.[214]

[Inclosure No.2.]
HEADQUARTERS FORREST'S CAVALRY,
In the Field, June 23, 1864.
Maj. Gen. C. C. WASHBURN,
Commanding U. S. Forces, Memphis, Tenn.:
GENERAL: Your communication of the 19th instant is received, in which you say "you are left in doubt as to the course the Confederate Government intends to pursue hereafter in regard to colored troops."

Allow me to say that this is a subject upon which I did not and do not propose to enlighten you. It is a matter to be settled by our Governments through their proper officers, and I respectfully refer you to them for a solution of your doubts. You ask me to state whether "I contemplate either their slaughter or their return to slavery." I answer that I slaughter no man except in open warfare, and that my prisoners, both white and black, are turned over to my Government to be dealt with as it may direct. My Government is in possession of all the facts as regards my official conduct and the operations of my command since I entered the service, and if you desire a proper discussion and decision, I refer you again to the President [Davis] of the Confederate States.

I would not have you understand, however, that in a matter of so much importance I am indisposed to place at your command and disposal any facts desired, when applied for in a manner becoming an officer holding your rank and position, for it is certainly desirable to every one occupying a public position to be placed right before the world, and there has been no time since the capture of Fort Pillow that I would not have furnished all the facts connected with its capture had they been applied for properly; but now the matter rests with the two Governments. I have, however, for your information, inclosed you copies of the official correspondence between the commanding officers at Fort Pillow and myself; also copies of a statement of Captain Young, the senior officer of that garrison, together with (sufficient) extracts from a report of the affair by my aide-de-camp, Capt. Charles W. Anderson, which I approve and indorse as correct.

Confederate Colonel
W. L. Duckworth.

As to the death of Major Bradford, I knew nothing of it until eight or ten days after it is said to have occurred. On the 13th (the day after the capture of Fort Pillow) I went to Jackson, and the report that I had of the affair was this: Major Bradford was with other officers sent to the headquarters of Colonel McCulloch, and all the prisoners were in charge of one of McCulloch's regiments. Bradford requested the privilege of attending the burial of his brother, which was granted, he giving his parole to return; instead of returning he changed his clothing and started for Memphis. Some of my men were hunting deserters, and came on Bradford just as he had landed on the south bank of Hatchie, and arrested him. When arrested he claimed to be a Confederate soldier belonging to Bragg's army; that he had been home on furlough, and was then on his way to join his command. As he could show no papers he was believed to be a deserter and was taken to Covington, and not until he was recognized and spoken to by citizens did the guards know that he was Bradford. He was sent by Colonel Duckworth, or taken by him, to Brownsville. All of Chalmers' command went south from Brownsville via La Grange, and as all the other prisoners had been gone some time, and there was no chance for them to catch up and place Bradford with them, he was ordered by Colonel Duckworth or General Chalmers to be sent to me at Jackson. I knew nothing of the matter until eight or ten days afterward. I heard that his body was found near Brownsville. I understand that he attempted to escape, and was shot. If he was improperly killed nothing would afford me more pleasure than to punish the perpetrators to the full extent of the law, and to show you how I regard such transactions I can refer you to my demand upon Major-General Hurlbut (no doubt upon file in your office) for the delivery to Confederate authorities of one Col. Fielding Hurst and others of his regiment, who deliberately took out and killed 7 Confederate soldiers, one of whom they left to die after cutting off his tongue, punching out his eyes, splitting his mouth on each side to his ears, and cutting off his privates.

I have mentioned and given you these facts in order that you may have no further excuse or apology for referring to these matters in connection with myself, and to evince to you my determination to do all in my power to avoid the responsibility of causing the adoption of the policy which you seem determined to press.

In your letter you acknowledge the fact that the negro troops did take an oath on bended knee to show no quarter to my men; and you say further, "you have no doubt they went to the battle-field expecting to be slaughtered," and admit also the probability of their having proclaimed on their line of march that no quarter would be shown us. Such being the case, why do you ask for the disavowal on the part of the commanding general of this department or the Government in regard to the loss of life at Tishomingo Creek? That your troops expected to be slaughtered, appears to me, after the oath they took, to be a very reasonable and natural expectation. Yet you, who sent them out, knowing and now admitting that they had sworn to such a policy, are complaining of atrocities, and demanding acknowledgments and disavowals on the part of the very men you went forth sworn to slay whenever in your power. I will in all candor and truth say to you that I had only heard these things, but did not believe them to be true; at any rate, to the extent of your admission; indeed, I did not attach to them the importance they deserved, nor did I know of the threatened vengeance, as proclaimed along their lines of march, until the contest was over. Had I and my men known it as you admit it, the battle of Tishomingo Creek would have been noted as the bloodiest battle of the war. That you sanctioned this policy is plain, for you say now "that if the negro is treated as a prisoner of war you will receive with pleasure the announcement, and will explain the fact to your colored troops at once, and desire (not order) that they recall the oath; but if they are either to be slaughtered or returned to slavery, let the oath stand."

Your rank forbids a doubt as to the fact that you and every officer and man of your department is identified with this policy and responsible for it, and I shall not permit you, notwithstanding, by your studied language in both your communications, you seek to limit the operations of your unholy scheme and visit its terrible consequences alone upon that ignorant, deluded, but unfortunate people, the negro, whose destruction you are planning in order to accomplish ours. The negroes have our sympathy, and so far as consistent with safety will spare them at the expense of those who are alone responsible for the inauguration of a worse than savage warfare.

Now, in conclusion, I demand a plain, unqualified answer to two questions, and then I have done with further correspondence with you on this subject. This matter must be settled. In battle and on the battle-field, do you intend to slaughter my men who fall into your hands? If you do not intend to do so, will they be treated as prisoners of war? I have over 2,000 of [Samuel D.] Sturgis' command prisoners, and will hold every officer and private as hostage until I receive your declarations and am satisfied that you carry out in good faith the answers you make, and until I am assured that no Confederate soldier has been foully dealt with from the day of the battle at Tishomingo Creek to this time. It is not yet too late for you to retrace your steps and arrest the storm.

Relying as I do upon that Divine Power which in wisdom disposes of all things; relying also upon the support and approval of my Government and countrymen, and the unflinching bravery and endurance of my troops, and with a consciousness that I have done nothing to produce, but all in my power consistent with honor and the personal safety of myself and command to prevent it, I leave with you the responsibility of bringing about, to use your own language, "a state of affairs too fearful for contemplation."
I am, general, very respectfully, yours, &c.,
N. B. FORREST, Major-General.[215]

On June 17, 1864, just days prior to these communications between the two generals, Washburn had also contacted General Stephen D. Lee, "asking for information as to the intention of the

Confederates concerning colored soldiers who might fall into their hands as prisoners of war." June 28 Lee sent Washburn the following reply:

> The version [of Fort Pillow] given by you and your Government is untrue, and not sustained by the facts to the extent that you indicate. The garrison was summoned in the usual manner, and its commanding officer assumed the responsibility of refusing to surrender after having been informed by General Forrest of his ability to take the fort, and of his fears as to what the result would be in case the demand was not complied with. The assault was made under a heavy fire and with considerable loss to the attacking party. Your colors were never lowered, and your garrison never surrendered, but retreated under cover of a gun-boat with arms in their hands and constantly using them. This was true particularly of your colored troops, who had been firmly convinced by your teachings of the certainty of slaughter in case of capture. Even under these circumstances, many of your men, white and black, were taken prisoners. I respectfully refer you to history for numerous cases of indiscriminate slaughter after successful assault, even under less aggravated circumstances. It is generally conceded by all military precedent that where the issue had been fairly presented and the ability displayed, fearful results are expected to follow a refusal to surrender.
>
> The case under consideration is almost an extreme one. You had a servile race armed against their masters, and in a country which had been desolated by almost unprecedented outrages. I assert that our officers, with all the circumstances against them, endeavored to prevent the effusion of blood, and as an evidence of this I refer you to the fact that both white and colored prisoners were taken, and are now in our hands.[216]

Forrest's battlefield tactics rightfully earned him the title: "The greatest cavalry officer of the War, on either side."

8

FORT PILLOW IN SUMMATION

A REVIEW OF THE BATTLE & FORREST'S ROLE

IN THE FINAL ANALYSIS, IF Forrest had truly wanted to "massacre" every last Yankee at Fort Pillow, a mere word from him to his men would have easily accomplished this order in but a short time.[217] Indeed, a complete capture of the garrison could have been executed by Forrest's sharpshooters alone, without any need for an assault by storm.[218] The bold fact remains that 60 percent of the Union soldiers survived, hardly what one would call a massacre.[219]

General Forrest after the War.

Actually, Forrest and his soldiers fought in a professional and reasonable manner over an eight-hour period, giving the Yanks plenty of opportunities to either fight their way out or surrender. Forrest should not be blamed because they succeeded at neither. Instead, he should be hailed as a hero for ridding the fort of its "nest" of Yankee bullies, swindlers, bandits, criminals, hustlers, bummers, thieves, rapists, sadists, psychopaths, and murderers, or what Forrest called "a motley herd of negroes, traitors, and Yankees."[220]

And what about those African-American Yanks who were among

the 40 percent who perished? Some estimate their individual casualty rate at about 64 percent.[221] Why so high compared to the whites?

Careful research proves that they were certainly not the victims of systemized racial butchery inside the fort, as South-haters wildly claim. The reality is that most of them died during the fighting that took place *outside* the fort, under the bluffs and in the surrounding waters. Also, many of them, being drunk and feeling quite invincible, refused to surrender. These men were shot down in isolated events during the first morning wave of Confederate assaults on the fort, finally perishing near or in the river. Had Forrest and his men been acting out of racial animosity, as Northern myth claims, every single black Union soldier would have died.[222] Considering the number who survived, as well as those who were captured, under the complex conditions at Fort Pillow on April 12, 1864, it would be more accurate to say that the Rebels went out of their way *not* to massacre African-Americans that day.

The Federal investigative committee that later tried to indict Forrest for "war crimes" at the fort had few scruples and a clear anti-Forrest agenda, and was no doubt intended to aid Lincoln's anti-South propaganda efforts.[223] Naturally it failed in its goal, for it had rested its case on "extravagant," highly dubious, contradictory, inconsistent, obviously erroneous, even inadmissible "evidence"[224]—much of it hearsay and gross exaggeration,[225] and most of it collected long after the event occurred;[226] the "written" testimony of illiterate soldiers; and "eyewitnesses" who were nowhere near the fort during the battle. Indeed, the entire charade was based on the charge that a "slaughter" had occurred "after surrender," a surrender itself that never took place.[227]

Among the interviews procured during the investigation was one between the Yankee committee members and a black man named Jacob Thompson:

> U.S. Government Committee: Did you see any rebel officers about there when this [the "massacre"] was going on?
> Thompson: Yes, sir; old Forrest was one.
> U.S. Government Committee: Did you know Forrest?
> Thompson: Yes, sir; he was a little bit of a man. I had seen him before at Jackson.
> U.S. Government Committee: Are you sure he was there when this was going on?

Thompson: Yes, sir.[228]

Referring to the enormously powerful, muscularly intimidating, 6 foot, 2 inch Forrest as "a little bit of a man" must have garnered a chuckle, even from the Union committee members! It was, in part, obvious fictitious "testimonies" such as this that finally discredited the groups' investigation.

Additionally, it will be remembered, Forrest, atypically in this case, did not lead the charge at Fort Pillow. Having been injured from a falling horse, he was 400 yards to the rear for much of the conflict, and left the scene of the battle as soon as it was over, long before nightfall. So it would have been virtually impossible for Jacob Thompson, or anyone else, to have seen Forrest anywhere near the fort.

It was more than obvious, even to many Northerners at the time, that the charges against Forrest were absurd, false, and villainous.[229] Despite leading questions, ignorant "eyewitnesses," and a fully biased court, eventually honest and trustworthy soldiers (from both sides) who were actually at the scene attested to Forrest's innocence, and the U.S. government took him off their list of suspects.[230] In the end, not one of the five charges of the committee's report could withstand a detailed examination of the facts.[231]

For the benefit of history, two of the Yankees who attested to Forrest's innocence deserve special mention. Unsurprisingly, both were African-Americans.

The first, a black Union private named Ellis Falls, said that without a doubt Forrest had commanded his men to "stop fighting" when it seemed things were about to get out of control.[232] The second, a black Union private named Major Williams, heard a Confederate yell out during the battle that Forrest did *not* want any blacks killed; that they were to be captured and returned to their owners.[233]

As is typical of Northern myth, Forrest, the inevitable Southern scapegoat, takes the blame for everything that happened at Fort Pillow. But what about the Yanks? Are none of them to be held accountable? Either Booth or Bradford could have surrendered. Indeed, under the circumstances (an indefensible fort against an overpowering enemy), they should have. They had nothing to fear as Forrest had promised to treat all those captured, both white and black, as prisoners of war.[234]

Confederate Captain W. A. Goodman, who served under General Chalmers, and who was the purveyor of several notes that passed between Forrest and the Yanks at Fort Pillow, later recalled:

> I have no copy . . . of any of the correspondence that ensued, before me, but I am satisfied that my recollection of the substance of the different notes is correct; and I remember the proposition in the first to treat the garrison as prisoners of war, provided they were surrendered, the more clearly because, when the note was handed to me, there was some discussion about it among the officers present, and it was asked whether it was intended to include the negro soldiers as well as the white; to which both General Forrest and General Chalmers replied, that it was so intended; and that if the fort was surrendered, the whole garrison, white and black, should be treated as prisoners of war. No doubt as to the meaning and scope of this proposition was ever expressed or intimated in any of the notes and conversations which followed it under the flag of truce.[235]

Confederate Sergeant Richard R. Hancock.

We must also consider that Bradford allowed his men to drink, become inebriated, and harass and mock the Confederates. Completely mismanaging his command, he disregarded Forrest's promise to treat both whites and blacks as prisoners of war, delayed the inevitable surrender, ignored a flag of truce, neglected to wave off approaching Union gunboats, then failed to raise a signal flag that would have told the steamers that a truce was under discussion—a "perfect storm" of factors that could only lead to one thing: the disaster that followed.[236]

And what about the Union president? Does he not bear some of the responsibility for the deaths of the black Yankees at Fort Pillow? As even Northern abolitionists complained at the time, Lincoln treated black Union soldiers with obvious contempt and racial prejudice, not only referring to them as an inferior race[237] (using the "n" word)[238] and segregating them, but also refusing to grant them the protection of citizenship or the right to vote. Why should the soldiers in Forrest's command have been expected to treat them any better?[239]

Former black servant and sagacious abolitionist, author, and orator, Frederick Douglass, was horrified by the white racism he saw in Lincoln's armies. Searching for the cause he eventually had to concede that as a fish rots from the head down, the trouble lay with white racist, white supremacist, white separatist, Lincoln himself—the same man who said: "What I would most desire would be the separation of the white and black races."[240] "Why should negroes enlist when the U.S. military and you, its commander-in-chief, are so prejudiced against them?" Douglass asked the Yankee president rhetorically.[241]

While Yankee and New South historians delight in regaling their readers with the fairy tale of the "Fort Pillow Massacre," they conveniently gloss over authentic incidents in which black Union soldiers massacred white Confederate soldiers. One of the more notable of these occurred at Fort Blakely, Alabama, where, without orders, black Federal troops charged a Rebel stronghold and mercilessly slaughtered surrendering white soldiers. The white Yankee officers in command had little sympathy for their white counterparts from the South, noting the fact that even though the Rebs had tried to surrender, nothing could have saved them from being cut down and slaughtered by "our niggers." Even black leaders, such as Chaplain Henry M. Turner, were horrified by such wanton mass murders.[242]

THE SOUTH RESTS HER CASE

In all actuality, Fort Pillow embodies one of the true and great ironies of the "Civil War": while Forrest's name has long been associated with racism and violent atrocities at the battle, it has been repeatedly proven that he and his men were completely innocent of any and all such accusations. This is why Forrest could publically state, with a clear conscience, that "I have no explanations, apologies, or disavowals to make . . ." Yet, the Yankee soldiers at Fort Pillow, who committed assaults, burglary, rape, and even murder upon the local citizenry over a period of many months, are held up as paragons of virtue and the "innocent victims of Southern brutality." And they call Southern history a "lie"!

Former Northern slave Frederick Douglass was appalled by Lincoln's racism, stating publicly that the Yankee president's attitude toward African-Americans lacked "the genuine spark of humanity."

In his letter to President Andrew Johnson after the War, Forrest voiced his final thoughts on the entire matter. "As a Confederate soldier and officer," he wrote, "I feel completely justified concerning the attack on Fort Pillow. Rational individuals will never be taken in by the leading questions and thoroughly inculcated 'witnesses' called forth by the U.S. committee assigned to investigate the battle," Forrest went on to note.[243]

Millions of Southerners understood and agreed. One of them, William Witherspoon,[244] one of Forrest's cavalrymen, spoke for many when he wrote in 1910 that "the Yankee version of what occurred at Fort Pillow is nothing remotely similar to what actually took place. We Southerners have already expressed more than enough regret," Witherspoon declared, "and the truth is that no apology is needed—not now or in the future."[245]

In 1868, echoing Witherspoon, Jordan and Pryor wrote:

> We submit to the candid and those who are capable of accepting the truth that, in what occurred after the Confederates stormed the trenches, there was neither cruel purpose nor cruel negligence of duty, neither intention nor inadvertence, on the part of General Forrest, whose course, therefore, stands utterly devoid of the essence of rage or wrong.[246]

In 1866 one of the South's greatest champions, Edward A. Pollard, offered his summary of the battle:

> In the capture of Fort Pillow the list of casualties embraced five hundred out of a garrison of seven hundred; and the enemy entitled the affair "The Fort Pillow Massacre," and Northern newspapers and Congressional committees circulated absurd stories about negro troops being buried alive. The explanation of the unusual

proportion of carnage is simple. After the Confederates got into the fort, the Federal flag was not hauled down; there was no surrender; relying upon his gunboats in the river, the enemy evidently expected to annihilate Forrest's forces after they had entered the works; and so the fighting went on to the last extremity. Some of the negro troops, in their cowardice, feigned death, falling to the ground, and were either pricked up by the bayonet, or rolled into the trenches to excite their alarm—to which circumstance is reduced the whole story of "burying negroes alive." Forrest was a hard fighter; he had an immense brain; but he knew but little about grammar and dictionaries. In describing the alarm and bewilderment in Fort Pillow to a superiour officer—who, by the way, has frequently expressed the opinion that Forrest, notwithstanding his defects in literary education, stood second only to Stonewall Jackson as the most remarkable man of the war,—Forrest said: "General, the damned Yankees kept firing horizontally right up into the air."[247]

An Atlanta newspaper also defended Forrest's actions at Fort Pillow, stating that "the General's wartime bravery, which was manifestly apparent on countless bloody fields, will certainly and eventually persuade the world that such a man completely lacks the ability to commit the crimes and atrocities for which he has been unfairly charged."[248]

In a word, there is not a single shred of incontestable evidence that Forrest was guilty of anything at Fort Pillow,[249] as even the most scurrilous anti-Forrest supporters must now admit. Yet, since his exact role will never be fully known,[250] he will forever remain a target of South-haters who feel free to fill in the missing pages with whatever slur, lie, or fable they choose to invent.

All the anti-Forrest vitriol in the world, however, does not make the General guilty. If anything, it only further proves his innocence. As John Allan Wyeth remarked in 1899 concerning the story of the so-called "Fort Pillow massacre":

> There is an adage that in war as in love all means of accomplishing the end desired are permissible. In the crisis of a great civil war, when each side was bending every energy for success, the leaders of the opposing forces justified a resort to measures of diplomacy in order to weaken their antagonists which a strict construction of right and truth would not have allowed. The proclamation of

emancipation may be mentioned as such a measure—the unlawful and unjust sweeping away of private property.

The refusal of the United States Government to exchange prisoners, thus condemning to a lingering death those of its own and its enemy's soldiers, was a war measure. In this same category should be placed the report of the Congressional Committee upon the capture of Fort Pillow, and the story of a massacre which was deftly woven out of the exaggerated testimony of two or three of the officers and some of the negroes and whites who were of the garrison, much of which testimony was so self-contradicting as to prove its falsity, and all of which was *ex parte* and inadequate in establishing the trumped-up charges of a violation of the rules governing civilized warfare.

Forrest had become a man of great importance in the mighty struggle the South was making. The opportunity which now presented itself to injure his reputation and blacken his character and that of his men was not to be lost.

To further excite the indignation of the Northern people and of the civilized world, by the wide publication of a horrible story of massacre which could not be refuted before it had done irreparable damage to the cause of the South, and further to impress upon the minds of the negroes who were then flocking to the ranks of the Union army that in future battles they could not expect quarter, and must therefore fight with desperation to the last, was a stroke of policy the advantage of which the shrewd politicians at Washington did not intend to lose.[251]

The End

APPENDICES

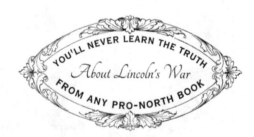

YOU'LL NEVER LEARN THE TRUTH
About Lincoln's War
FROM ANY PRO-NORTH BOOK

APPENDIX A

"THE TRUE STORY OF FORT PILLOW"

BY MAJOR CHARLES W. ANDERSON, STAFF OFFICER UNDER GENERAL FORREST

While I have spent many years carefully researching the subject of Forrest and the Battle of Fort Pillow, and have concluded that the General is innocent of all wrongdoing, one need not take my word for it alone. Far more persuasive is the fact that we have numerous eyewitness accounts from reputable individuals who were at the scene. One of these was Forrest's aide-de-camp and assistant inspector-general, Major Charles W. Anderson, whose unimpeachable testimony appeared in the November 1895 issue of *Confederate Veteran* magazine. Below is Major Anderson's in-depth description of the conflict, which is followed by a second on-site report, that of Confederate Sergeant Richard R. Hancock. — Lochlainn Seabrook, 2015

A fter the return of Gen. Forrest's command from his expedition to Paducah, Ky., his Adjutant General, Major [John P.] Strange, was attacked with hemorrhage of the lungs, and when ready for the move against Fort Pillow his condition was so critical that Gen. Forrest thought it best to leave Col. [M. C.] Galloway and his son, [William] Willie Forrest, at Jackson with him; hence, I was the only staff officer with Gen. Forrest in his expedition against that fort.

Gen. [James R.] Chalmers, with [Tyree H.] Bell's and [Robert] McCulloch's brigades, and four small pieces of artillery, moved out from Jackson on the morning of the 10th of April, 1864. Gen. Forrest, with escort, and a detachment under Lieut. Col. [D. M.] Wisdom, followed later. On reaching Brownsville he directed Gen. Chalmers to make a forced march on the night of the 11th, and if possible to reach Fort Pillow by or before day on the morning of the 12th (in order to take the garrison by surprise), and to attack at once on arrival.

Gen. Forrest rested a few hours at Brownsville, and followed Chalmers. When within eight or ten miles of the river we heard the first cannonading at the fort, and knew then that Gen. Chalmers was at work.

Our march was quickened, and some three or four miles from the fort we were met by a courier with a dispatch from Gen. Chalmers, stating that he had driven the enemy into their works and the rifle pits around the fort, and, as I now remember, expressing the opinion that they could not be assaulted and captured except with heavy cost. This dispatch put us in a trot, and Gen. Forrest was soon on the ground and in command.

As everything was comparatively quiet, our jaded horses were rested for a few moments, while the General held a short conference with Gen. Chalmers. After which, unaccompanied except by myself, he made a rapid circuit around the land side of the fort from the Federal horse lot to Coal [Cold] Creek above, returning to our starting point over a diminished distance from the works. In returning we were subjected to a constant and dangerous fire from the parapets. The General's horse was wounded, and my own pulled up dead lame after leaping a small ditch. I supposed him shot also, but it proved a strain. Going at once to the Escort's position in rear of the Federal horse lot, I dismounted private Lucas, of that company, took his horse, and rejoined the General as he was returning alone from a re-examination of the ground over which we had ridden, and as we galloped rapidly around and down toward the river, a second horse was shot under him and killed.

In these examinations he found a ravine almost encircling the fort, and that from the high ground over which we had ridden sharpshooters could command most of the area inside the fort, and could enfilade its retreating angles, and render them untenable or the occupation exceedingly hazardous. He also discovered that the ravine once gained by our troops, they would be just as well fortified as were the enemy, one party being inside and the other just outside of the same earthworks. His plan of action was quickly determined, was speedily communicated to Gen. Chalmers, and by him to his brigade commanders, and preparations and dispositions made at once for its execution.

Under signals from the fort, the gunboat *New Era* lay abreast of the mouth of the ravine below the fort, and was constantly shelling us. By the General's directions, I moved to the high bluff below the mouth of the ravine, where a plunging fire would necessarily drive her from her position. Of this movement she was doubtless advised by signal from the fort, as she steamed up the river and out of range before we could open fire on her.

While absent on this duty, strong lines of sharpshooters had been thrown forward to the high ground previously referred to, and when I rejoined the General our whole force, under a terrific fire from the artillery and small arms of the garrison, was closing rapidly around the works. Bell's brigade was on the right, extending from the mouth of Coal [Cold] Creek southward; McCulloch's brigade on the left, extending from the ravine below the fort northward, his right joining the left of Bell's line abreast of the fort.

When Gen. Chalmers had gained this desired position, which was done rapidly and handsomely, but with the loss of some brave officers and men, Gen. Forrest determined, in order to save further loss of life, to demand a surrender. He knew the place was practically in his possession, as the enemy could not depress their artillery so as to rake the slopes around the fort with grape and canister, and the constant and fatal fire of our sharpshooters forced the besieged to keep down behind their parapets. He believed the Federal commander fully recognized the situation, and that he would accept an offer to surrender in preference to an assault by a force much larger than his own, and in full view. Bugles were sounded for a truce and a parley, and a white flag sent forward with a demand for the immediate and unconditional surrender of all the Federal troops at Fort Pillow.

The smoke of approaching steamers ascending the river had been visible for some time. Three of them were now nearing the fort. Gen. Forrest ordered me to take a detachment from McCulloch's brigade and move to the bluff, and prevent them from landing. I at once detached three companies (about one hundred and fifty men) and moved them rapidly to a position within sixty yards of the south entrance of the fort, descending by a path and occupying some old rifle pits on the face of the bluff, which were built by the Confederates in 1861 for protecting their water battery. These pits were washed out, broken, and in many places filled in by caving banks from above, yet afforded some protection.

The channel of the Mississippi River at Fort Pillow runs close under the bluff, and as the foremost steamer neared our position I directed one of he men to fire at her pilot house. A second shot from another secured attention at once, and she sheared off toward the bar across the river. This steamer was the *Olive Branch*, crowded from forecastle to hurricane deck with Federal soldiers. She was closely followed by the *Hope*, and the *M. R. Cheek*, both of which adopted the course of the leading steamer, making for the bar on the west side of the river, and all of them passing up to the position of the gunboat *New Era*, which lay midstream just above the fort.

The bugler of the Thirteenth Tennessee Federal Cavalry had taken advantage of the truce to recover his trappings from his horse, which he had left tied in a small gulch or ravine leading from the fort toward the river. As I rode to the head of it I discovered him, with his back to me, busily engaged in securing his gum cloth and coat. I waited quietly until he turned to regain the fort. His astonishment and trepidation can well be imagined at finding a six shooter levelled at his face and an able bodied "Reb" behind it. Ordering him to hand me is carbine butt end foremost, and then to untie his horse and lead him out ahead of me, I rode down, and around to the General's position, who was then with much impatience awaiting an answer to his final demand for a surrender.

As there were no steamers in sight coming from below, I remained with him until the final and emphatic refusal of the garrison to surrender was received.

I had in the meantime communicated to him the position of the gunboat, also that two large empty barges were cabled to the shore in rear of the fort, which might be utilized by the garrison, under her protecting fire, as a means of escape. I was equally particular in impressing upon him the hazardous position of the detachment on the face of the bluff, (out of sight of, and entirely separated from, the balance of the command), and that in the event of any failure to carry the works by assault, a sortie from the south entrance of the fort in their rear, with the gunboat and its cannon and marines in their front, their destruction or capture would certainly follow.

He fully recognized their isolated and exposed position, but, ignoring the contingency, he directed me to return to my position at once—to take no part in the assault, but to prevent any escape from the garrison by barges or otherwise—to pour rifle balls into the open ports of the *New Era* when she went into action, and, to use his last expression, "fight everything 'blue' between wind and water until yonder flag comes down."

Returning at once, all necessary orders were given to the senior officer of the detachment, and by him they were passed along the trenches. I took a position in speaking distance of him, and where, by remaining mounted, I could see the fort flag; preferring to expose myself and horse to the expected fire of the *New Era* to that from the parapets of the fort; from which I was not fifty yards distant, but fully protected by an intervening ridge, around the head of which I had intercepted the bugler.

From this position I had a full view of the entire water line in rear of the fort, and much of the sloping bank above it. Owing to the conformation of the bluff, its brow in the rear of the fort was not visible, but nearly all the slope from the water line to within twenty or thirty feet of the top of the bluff in the rear of the fort was in plain view.

This was the situation as taken in while anxiously awaiting the sound of [Jacob] Gaus' well-known bugle. It soon came; was repeated along the line, and at once followed by the yells of our men, and a terrific discharge of the batteries and small arms of the fort. In a few moments a portion of the garrison rushed down toward the river, and upon them we opened a destructive fire. The yells of our troops as they mounted the parapets could be plainly heard above the din and rattle of musketry, and in a moment more the whole force of the garrison came rushing down the bluff toward the water with arms in hand, but only to fall thick and fast from the short range fire of the detachment temporarily under my command, which threw them into unutterable dismay and confusion. This fire, with that of the whole assaulting line, was, for the few moments it lasted, most destructive and deadly. The moment the Federal colors came down, I ordered firing to cease at once, and it was promptly done. Directing the commanding officer to bring his men up out of the pits and report to his regiment, I dashed into the south entrance of the fort. Everything was in confusion and the dead and wounded were lying thick around, but there was no firing anywhere.

I met the General between the flagstaff and the entrance, and his first words were: "Major, we drove them right to you, and I cut their flag down as soon as I could get to it."

No one under such circumstances could accurately give the time of these transactions, but I am satisfied in my own mind that it was less than fifteen minutes from the time our bugles sounded until their colors came down, and less than two minutes from the time they were lowered until firing had ceased, and I had joined the General inside the works.

Every soldier who has ever participated in work of this kind knows that such actions must be short, sharp and desperate, to be successful.

Gen. Forrest's first order was to wheel around and move out the cannon of the fort so as to command the river. He could have opened fire at long range upon the *New Era*, as she steamed away up the river, but instead of doing so, directed me to take Capt. Young, the Federal provost marshal, and a white flag, and endeavor to open communication with her, with a view of delivering the Federal wounded and securing surgical aid for them until they could be removed.

With a flag we followed her up the river bank, waving her to stop and send a boat ashore. She paid no attention whatever to our signals. Doubtless her commander thought our flag a ruse to effect his capture, and his vessel soon disappeared around the point above the fort.

Returning and reporting to the General our failure to communicate with the *New Era*, he at once caused details to be made of all the unwounded Federals, under their own officers, to first bring into the huts and houses on the hill all their wounded comrades, and then to proceed at once to bury their dead.

When the wounded and dead had been removed from the face of the bluff, a detail of our own men was sent down to gather up all the small arms thrown down by the garrison. I went with this detail myself, and inspected and handed over to our ordinance officer two hundred and sixty-nine rifles and six cases of rifle ammunition, all of which were gathered up on the face of the slope from the fort to the water's edge. The six cases of cartridges were piled against the upturned roots of an old tree, with their tops removed, ready for immediate distribution and use.

Gen. Forrest remained on the ground until late in the evening, hoping to be able to deliver the wounded to some steamer, should any approach the fort; but as none ventured to come in sight, he gave full directions to and turned over the command to Gen. Chalmers, and, moving out on the Brownsville road with his escort, we encamped at a farm house about seven or eight miles from Fort Pillow.

As we were mounting our horses next morning (the 13th) en route to Jackson, a heavy cannonading began at the fort. The General at once directed me to take ten men from the escort and, with Capt. Young (who was still with us), to proceed back to Fort Pillow and again attempt negotiation with the Federal fleet for the removal of their wounded.

On arrival I caused all of Gen. Chalmers' details, at whom the gunboats were firing, to be at once withdrawn, and accompanied by Capt. Young only, with a white flag, rode down to the water's edge. The gunboat *Silver Cloud* discovered us and our flag, ceased firing, and steamed slowly in shore. When within hailing distance her engines were stopped, and her commander, through his trumpet asked, "What was wanted?" I asked him to send an officer ashore, and I would deliver my communications in writing. Seeing him run out and launch a small boat into the river, I dismounted from my horse and wrote briefly what was desired; but, on turning around, found the small boat nearing our position with the United States flag at its bow and six armed marines and an officer aboard. Waving him back, and calling his attention to our white flag, I told him that I could hold no parley with him until he returned to his vessel, hoisted a white flag, and returned with his oarsmen unarmed. This he readily did, and on his return a communication was given him, requesting the landing of the *Silver Cloud* in order to negotiate for a truce, and for the delivery of all the wounded of the garrison. and assuring the commander of his safety in landing under a white flag; but, if unwilling to land, to send a boat back and I would go on board to complete the desired arrangements.

As soon as my message was delivered, Capt. Ferguson lowered his colors, ran up a white flag and landed his vessel. Going on board, I was furnished by the purser with pen and paper, and in a short time an agreement was made for a truce from 9 o'clock A.M. to 5 o'clock P.M. All the conditions named were accepted by Capt. Ferguson, and the articles drawn up in duplicate and signed by both parties; after which I went ashore, sending a dispatch at once to Gen. Chalmers' headquarters, notifying him of the truce, and that, for fear of a collision, none of his troops must be allowed to come within the old Confederate rifle entrenchments, but suggesting that he and staff come down whenever his duties would permit. I then sent four of my men to clear the fort and its surroundings of all stragglers, and to allow no one to remain on the grounds but surgeons and their assistants.

Allowing time for the men to carry out these orders, I notified Capt. Ferguson to run out his stagings, and that the fort and all its surroundings were now in his possession. Several steamers were in sight awaiting developments and signals. They were signalled to drop down and land, and in a short time the removal of the wounded to the steamer *Platte Valley* began.

I remained at her gangways, taking a full and complete list of the wounded as they were carried on board, placing a guard at the stage planks of the other steamers, to insure the delivery of all the wounded upon one vessel.

Capt. Young, who was left ashore in charge of Sergt. Eaton, of the escort, learned that his wife was on one of the steamers just landed, that she was in great stress of mind as to his fate, and asked permission (under guard) to go on board, assure her of his safety, give some instructions as to his private affairs, and bid her farewell. I placed him under parole of honor to report back to me at 2:30 P.M., and allowed him to go at once. He accepted the parole, with many thanks for my kindness, and reporting promptly at the designated hour, was sent out to Gen. Chalmers' headquarters to join his comrades as a prisoner of war.

Permission was given to all the passengers on the three steamers to visit the fort, and all of them did so, many of them bringing back in their hands buckles, belts, balls, buttons, etc., picked up on the rounds, which they requested permission to carry with them as relics or mementoes of Fort Pillow. All such requests were cheerfully and pleasantly granted.

Gen. Chalmers and staff came down and remained an hour or more, and notified me that he was withdrawing his command to Brownsville, and offering to leave a detachment to accompany me after the truce, which I declined, because I thought we could soon overtake them. With the prisoners and fort artillery I thought they could not move very rapidly. I did not knew then that one brigade and the prisoners and artillery were already half way to Brownsville, or I would most certainly have accepted a stronger escort.

Before the expiration of the truce all the wounded had been placed on the *Platte Valley*, and a receipt in duplicate taken from them, signed by Capt. Ferguson, of the *Silver Cloud*. I was, as may be well imagined, worn down and exhausted, and when my duties were over a couple of lieutenants of the Federal army on the *Platte Valley* insisted on my taking a parting glass with them at the bar of that steamer, which I, of course, did little thinking at the time that my acceptance of their hospitality and their courtesy would cost them heir commissions. For this courtesy and kindness, one officer was cashiered and the other reduced to the ranks.

A while before five o'clock I suggested to Capt. Ferguson the departure of the passenger steamers yet at the landing, and stated to him that after the truce I should proceed to burn all the buildings at Fort Pillow; that they had been preserved for the accommodation of the Federal wounded, and their existence was no longer necessary or desirable. When the steamers had all left, I assured Capt. Ferguson that there was no Confederate force within two miles of the fort, and that he could let go his lines and depart at his leisure, and without fear of molestation.

I then saluted him an adieu, and with my little squad rode slowly up the bluff.

The men with me were dismounted, and set to work scattering and distributing loose straw, hospital beds and bunks through all the buildings. We waited until the *Silver Cloud* let go her ties and swung out into the river. As she lowered her white flag the torch was applied, and as he ran up her colors the last buildings left at Fort Pillow burst into flames. We then mounted our horses and bade Fort Pillow a lasting adieu.

CONCLUDING COMMENTS BY MAJ. ANDERSON

The fearful loss of life at Fort Pillow is alone chargeable to the total incapacity of its commanding officer, and to the fatal and delusive promise or agreement made by Capt. Marshall, of the gunboat *New Era*, with Maj. Bradford—that is, that when whipped the garrison was to drop down under the bluff, and the *New Era* would give the rebels cannister and protect and succor them. Maj. Booth, who commanded Fort Pillow, was killed early in the morning by a bullet through the brain. His death placed the command in the hands of Maj. W. F. Bradford, of the Thirteenth Tennessee Federal Cavalry, a man without any military capacity whatever; and, if reports were true of him, his conduct as a soldier, as well as the violation of his parole after capture, show him as destitute of honor as wanting in military skill and ability.

When he found himself surrounded by a force thrice his own, and knew that his works were no longer defensible against an assault by such numbers, his plain duty was to surrender the fort and save further loss of life. Nor can he be excused for relying upon the promise of Capt. Marshall, after seeing and knowing that the movement of two howitzers to the low bluff had driven the *New Era* from the only position in which her promised aid could have been at all available.

Marshall did know, and Maj. Bradford ought to have known, that with the channel of the river right under the bluff, and a broad bar with shallow water right opposite the fort, the *New Era* could not get sufficient "offing" to elevate her guns and do any damage to parties on top of a bluff at least eighty feet above the water line.

Yet, with all this, the sequel shows that Maj. Bradford, relying upon the promise of Capt. Marshall, refused the third and last demand of Gen. Forrest for his surrender; and when assaulted and driven from the works, he retreated with arms in hands, and ammunition provided and placed under the bluff, only to find that the *New Era*, instead of dropping down and giving the Rebels grape and canister, steamed quickly out of harm's way, leaving the duped commander and the deluded garrison to their fate.

How far Capt. Marshall could have aided the garrison no one can say, but it would have been far better for his name and fame had be moved his vessel promptly into action, and perished in attempting to do as he promised, than live and know that his violated promise, and his abandonment of the garrison, first led and then left hundreds of his countrymen and comrades to a swift and sweeping destruction.

I have never hesitated to assert, as I do now, that, numbers considered, the detachment temporarily under my command did, by far, the most fatal and destructive, as well as the very last firing done at Fort Pillow. It was enfilading, a terribly short rifle range, and began with the retreat of the very first troops that left the fort, and continued steadily and rapidly until the Federal flag came down. In our position under, or on the face of the bluff, one could only know when the fort was in our possession by the falling of its colors or a special messenger. The former was the quicker, and under my orders, as soon as it fell, firing was promptly stopped, and, ordering the detachment to report back at once to its regiment, I was with the General in less than two minutes after the flag came down.

The charges against Gen. Forrest and his men of massacre and butchery at Fort Pillow are outrageously unjust and unfounded. He did every thing in his power to induce a surrender and avoid an assault. Thrice was a surrender demanded, and as often refused. There never was any surrender, therefore no massacre after surrender, as has been so erroneously and widely charged.

I take occasion here to say that in my long service with Gen. Forrest, his kindness to the vanquished, the unarmed and unresisting foe, was a marked characteristic of the man. He believed and always said and felt, that "war meant fight, and fight meant to kill," but never in all his career did a Federal soldier throw down his arms and surrender, that did not receive at once his consideration and protection. He captured many thousand Federals, and there is not one living to-day who can truthfully say that he was ever mistreated or ever insulted by Nathan Bedford Forrest. — Chas. W. Anderson.[252]

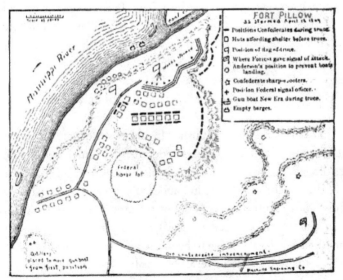

Illustration accompanying Major Anderson's description of the Battle of Fort Pillow April 12, 1864, on the Mississippi River at Henning, Tennessee.

APPENDIX B

AN EYEWITNESS ACCOUNT OF
THE BATTLE OF FORT PILLOW

FROM THE DIARY OF CONFEDERATE SERGEANT RICHARD R. HANCOCK,
COMPANY C, SECOND TENNESSEE CAVALRY, 1887

Monday, April 11th, 1864:

Forrest, leaving Jackson that morning, overtook Chalmers at Brownsville at two P.M., and ordered that officer to push ahead with the troops by a forced march, so that they might be in close proximity to Fort Pillow by daylight the next morning. The distance was thirty-eight miles. It was raining, and so dense was the darkness after midnight that it was difficult to distinguish the road or "to see a file-leader."

Tuesday, April 12th, 1864:

Nevertheless, onward and onward pushed Chalmers—with McCulloch's Brigade still in advance—and just before dawn on Tuesday, April 12th, his advance guard surprised the Federal pickets and captured all except one or two, who, escaping to the fort just at sunrise, gave the first warning of the danger impending. Thus Bell's Brigade had made the trip from Eaton to Fort Pillow—about seventy miles—in thirty hours. McCulloch's men had decidedly the advantage of Bell's, from the fact that by getting well on their way Sunday they got to rest Sunday night, while . . . Bell's men were in the saddle nearly all night, and then also Monday and Monday night, resulting in many of Bell's men being made sick.

Fort Pillow, first established in 1861 by the State of Tennessee, and still better fortified by the Confederate States Engineers, under the orders of General Beauregard, in March and April, 1862, is on the east bank of the Mississippi River, in Lauderdale County, some three and a half miles above Fulton, and just below the mouth of Coal [Cold] Creek. The lines of works erected by the Confederates were upon a very extended scale—far too large to be of the least use or value to a garrison so small as that which the Federals habitually kept there, therefore they had freshly thrown up breastworks upon the highest part—perhaps fifty feet above the water level— of a bank or bluff which extended for several hundred yards nearly parallel with the river, leaving a space, comparatively level, between its base and the river bank proper, perhaps thirty to fifty yards wide. The fort was near the southern extremity of this bluff, it being the highest, and about seventy-five yards from the river. About one acre of land was inclosed by earth works thrown up on three sides—north, south, and east. The wall was about eight feet high, exterior to which there was a ditch six feet deep and twelve feet broad. Eastward there was a gradual slope from the fort for from forty to fifty yards, when the descent became sudden into a narrow gorge which, extending northward four or five hundred yards, thence westward to Coal [Cold] Creek, thus separated the bluff upon which the fort stood from a labyrinth of hills and ridges, divided from each other by a net-work of interlacing, narrow ravines, and this slope was broken by several crooked and deep gullies, affording well-covered approaches for an enemy to within thirty to one hundred yards of the fort. Southward, this eminence also fell off gently for about two hundred yards, and then rapidly into a narrow valley, the course of which was perpendicular to the river, and in which were a number of trading houses and other buildings known as the town. This slope was seamed by a ravine which gave hostile access to within one hundred and fifty yards of the southern face of the works. Between this ravine and the fort were three or four rows of tents and cabins, and rightward from these, stretched around to the north for some two hundred yards a rifle-pit along the eastern verge of the acclivity. The armament consisted of two ten-pounder Parrott rifled guns, two twelvepounder howitzers, and two six-pounder rifled-bore field pieces, and the whole garrison did not exceed five hundred and eighty men. One gunboat—*New Era*—was present and took part in the defense. The timber was cut down for several hundred yards in front of the fort.

Upon the capture of the pickets, McCulloch's Brigade was pressed rapidly on with instructions to take up a position southward of the fort, and as near as possible to the river bank and work; therefore, McCulloch soon seized a position with his left flank on the river bank, about half a mile southward of the fort, the remainder of his line disposed in the ravines extending around and toward the north-east, in close proximity to a high ridge upon which were the old Confederate works, the most elevated point of which was occupied at the time by a Federal detachment. He then and there came to a halt to wait for Bell's Brigade (which was about two miles from the fort when the Federal guns first opened, a little after sunrise) to come up and take position. As soon as up Wilson's Regiment of Bell's Brigade was deployed directly in front to occupy the close attention of the garrison by an immediate, vigorous skirmish, while Colonel Barteau led the Second Tennessee rightward, winding his way as best he could through the woods to Coal [Cold] Creek bottom, and there dismounting threw his men forward to a good position a few hundred yards north of the fort along the north-east face of a hill. From this position skirmishers were thrown forward to brush the small force of Federal sharp-shooters back from their advanced positions; this drew the Federal guns from both fort and gunboat upon our position. Meanwhile Colonel Russell threw his regiment forward to a position between Barteau and Wilson. The investment was now complete, though it was at long range; and about this time, too (nine A.M.), General Forrest came upon the field, and about the same hour Major Booth, the Federal commander, and his adjutant by his side, were killed. Coming immediately to our position,[253] thence along the top of the bluff upon which the fort stood, General Forrest made as close an inspection of the fort and its surroundings as he possibly could, thus ascertaining that the conformation of the ground around the Federal works (as previously described) was such as to afford protection to his troops, while two ridges, from four to five hundred yards distant, eastward and north-eastward from the enemy's position, gave the Confederate sharp-shooters excellent cover, from which they completely commanded the interior of the Federal works, and might effectually silence their fire. He therefore decided at once to make a close investment, returned to our position and ordered Colonel Barteau to "move up." Accordingly the Second Tennessee "moved up" to the top of the bluff and opened fire upon the Federal garrison. By dropping over a little to the right and moving along the side of the bluff facing the river, it gave us some protection from the garrison, while at the same time this move placed us in easy range and plain view of the gunboat, which moved up as we moved down, and when about opposite to us she turned broadside as though she was going to give us "Hail Columbia;" however, after maneuvering around for a while, as though she was trying to scare us off of that bluff without firing a gun, she finally came to a halt several hundred yards above the fort, and (to our great relief) remained a "silent spectator" during the rest of the engagement.[254] Moving along this bluff to within about one hundred yards of the north side of the fort—perhaps some were nearer—Colonel Barteau halted and waited for the rest of the command to close up.

"The Confederates storming Fort Pillow."

After advancing a short distance with our regiment, Forrest turned and went round leftward to move up the rest of Bell's Brigade as well as McCulloch's. Accordingly Russell's and Wilson's Regiments were thrown forward, to the left of Barteau's, to a position in which their men were well sheltered by the conformation of the ground. McCulloch, advancing about the same time, soon brushed the Federals back from the old Confederate intrenchments, on the highest part of the ridge immediately in front of the south-eastern face of the work. The Federals fell back without further stand to their main work and the rifle-pit in its front, closely pressed by McCulloch, who seized and occupied the cluster of cabins on the southern face of the work, which were only about sixty yards from it, foiling an attempt on the part of the enemy to burn the buildings. He also carried and occupied the rifle-pit rightward, thus completing the investment at short range, extending from the river bank north of the fort to the river bank south. These positions thus secured were fatal to the defense, for the Confederates were now so placed that artillery could not be brought to bear upon them with much effect, except at a mortal exposure of the gunners, while rearward of the advance line were numerous sharp-shooters, favorably posted on several commanding ridges, ready to pick off any of the garrison showing their heads above, or, indeed, any men moving about within the circuit of, the parapets. Fully satisfied of his ability to carry the position without difficulty or delay, but desiring to avoid the loss of life that must occur in storming the works, Forrest determined to demand the surrender of the place. Accordingly, causing the signal for a cessation of hostilities to be given, he deputed Captain W. A. Goodman, Adjutant-General on the staff of General Chalmers, to bear a flag of truce with a formal demand in writing,[255] addressed to "Major L. F. Booth, commanding United States forces," as he was thought to be still in command. However, as we have seen, he had been dead for several hours, and the command had fallen into the feeble hands of W. F. Bradford, the commander of the odious Thirteenth Tennessee Battalion of Cavalry. Nevertheless, the answer received, after some delay, bore the name of Major L. F. Booth, and required an hour for consultation with his officers and those of the gunboat in regard to the demand for the surrender of his post and the vessel. On receiving this communication Forrest immediately replied, in writing, that he had not asked for, and did not expect, the surrender of the gunboat, but that of the fort and garrison, and that he would give twenty minutes for a decision. Moreover, so great was the animosity existing between the Tennesseans of the two commands, he added, that he could not be responsible for the consequences if obliged to storm the place.

During the period of the truce the smoke of several steamers[256] were discovered ascending the river; and speedily one crowded with troops, and her lower guards filled with artillery, was distinctly seen approaching, near at hand, and manifestly bearing directly for the beleaguered fortress. Apprehensive that an attempt would be made to land reinforcements from these steamers, Forrest promptly dispatched his aid-de-camp, Captain Anderson, with a squadron of McCulloch's Brigade, down to the river bank under the bluff and just below the southern face of the invested work. And the *Olive Branch*, in her course, soon came so near that by opening with a volley on the mass of men with whom she was laden a heavy loss of life must have been inflicted; but Captain Anderson, limiting himself strictly to preventing the landing of any reinforcements during the truce, caused two or three admonitory shots to be fired at the pilot-house, with the immediate effect of making her sheer off to the opposite shore, and pass on up the river.

Some minutes later the answer to the second demand was brought out of the fort and handed to Forrest by Captain Goodman. It ran as follows: "Your demand does not produce the desired effect." The Confederate General exclaimed: "This will not do; send it back, and say to Major Booth"—whose name was attached—"that I must have an answer in plain English—yes or no!" Captain Goodman returned not long after with the Federal answer, a brief but positive refusal to surrender the post. As soon as he had read this communication, turning to his staff and some officers around him, Forrest ordered that his whole force should be put in readiness for an immediate and simultaneous assault. After stimulating his troops with a few energetic words he, with a single bugler, rode to a commanding eminence, some four or five hundred yards east of the fort, from which he had a complete view of the field of operations, and, scanning the field, and observing that all was ready, caused the signal to be given for the resumption of hostilities; and at the first blare of the bugle the Confederate sharp-shooters, at all points, opened a galling fire upon the hostile parapet, to which the garrison replied for a few moments with great spirit. But so deadly was the aim of the Confederates from their enfilading positions that their enemies could not rise high enough from their scanty cover to fire over at their foes, nor use their artillery on the southern face without being shot down. Consequently there was practically little resistance, when, a few moments later, the bugle still sounding the charge, the main Confederate force, surging onward as with a single impulse, leaped headlong into the ditch, and, helping each other, they clambered nimbly, swiftly and simultaneously over the breastworks beyond, opening from its crest a fearful, converging fire, from all its forces, upon its garrison within.

In anticipation of this contingency Major Bradford, it appears, had arranged with the captain of the gunboat that, if beaten at the breastworks, the garrison would drop down under the bank and the gunboat would come to their succor and shelter them with its canister.

The prearranged signal was now given, and the whole garrison, white and black, for the most part with arms in their hands, broke for the place of refuge and naval aid there expected, leaving the Federal flag still aloft on its staff.[257] The gunboat, however, was recreant at this critical moment, and failed to give the least assistance; and no timely shower of canister came from its ports to drive back the Confederates, who swiftly and hotly followed after the escaping negroes and Tennesseans. As soon as we entered the fort two of the captured guns[258] were turned upon the gunboat, which caused her to move further up the river in place of coming to the relief of the garrison, as her commander had distinctly agreed to do. The left of the Second Tennessee entered the fort at the north-west corner, while the right extended westward down the bluff toward the river; and while they were pouring a volley into the right flank of the retreating Federals, the troops that had been stationed below the fort to watch the steamers did likewise for the enemy's left flank. Thus being exposed to a fire from both flanks, as well as rear, their ranks were fearfully thinned as they fled down that bluff toward the river. Finding that the succor which they had been promised from the gunboat was not rendered, nor at hand, they were greatly bewildered. Many threw themselves into the river and were drowned in their mad attempt to swim away from the direful danger which they apprehended; while others sought to escape along the river bank southward, as well as northward, and, still persisting in their efforts to get away, were shot or driven back. In the meantime, or as soon as he could reach the scene, Forrest, as well as Chalmers and other officers, interfered so energetically to stop the firing that it ceased speedily—ceased, in fact, within fifteen minutes from the time the bugle first sounded the charge. The garrison, as a whole, be it remembered, did not surrender at all. When we poured over, on all sides, into the work they did not yield—did not lay down their arms nor draw down their flag, but fled (some returning the fire of their pursuers) toward another position in which they were promised relief. Such was the animosity between the Tennesseans of the two commands, and as such is frequently the case in places taken by storm, some, no doubt, were shot after they had thrown down their arms and besought quarter; no such cases, however, happened to come under the immediate observation of the writer. The first order now issued by Forrest was to collect and secure the prisoners from possible injury, while details were made from them for the burial of the Federal dead. Among the prisoners taken unhurt was Major Bradford, the commanding officer of the post since nine in the morning, and at his special request Forrest ordered the Federal dead to be buried in the trenches of the work, the officers to be interred separately from their men.[259] Bradford was then temporarily paroled to supervise the burial of his brother, Captain Bradford, after which, under a pledge not to attempt to escape, he was placed for the night in the custody of Colonel McCulloch, who gave him a bed in his own quarters, and shared with him his supper. This pledge Major Bradford violated; taking advantage of the darkness and his knowledge of the locality, when his host was asleep, he effected his escape through the careless line of sentinels, and, in disguise, sought to reach Memphis.[260]

Among the prisoners taken was Captain Young, who with Captain Anderson, was sent up the river-side with a white flag to endeavor to open communication with the gunboat *New Era*, but every signal was obdurately ignored or disregarded, and keeping on her course she soon disappeared up the river. The object was to deliver into the hands of Captain Marshall, the commander of the *New Era*, as soon as possible, all the Federal wounded. As fast as possible, meanwhile, the wounded of both sides were gleaned from the bloody field and placed under shelter and the professional care of Confederate surgeons of the several regiments present.

This brilliant success was not achieved without severe loss on our part—the loss of some of our best soldiers. The whole command lost fourteen officers and men killed, and eighty-six wounded. Lieutenant George Leave (Company D, Second Tennessee), who was kind and generous as well as gallant and brave, fell mortally wounded by a canister-shot. Twelve more of our regiment besides Leave were wounded, four of them from Company C, as follows: W. L. Womack and Lieutenant H. L. W. Turney were slightly wounded, and C. E. Thomas and W. W. Hawkins severely. J. K. Dodd (Company D), William Duke and Nute Carr (Company E), John K. Brinkley and James Link (Company F), were among the wounded. William Duke's leg was broken near the ankle joint by a rifle-ball, and after examination and consultation our surgeons decided to amputate his foot. As soon as Duke learned their decision he called on D. B. Willard (a member of Company

C who had carried him from the field) to hand him his pistol, and said, "I'll shoot the first man who attempts to cut off my foot." "If you don't want it cut off it will not be done," said Willard. By request of Duke, Willard made some splinters, and finally the surgeons assisted in bandaging his leg, and the result was he soon got well, and thus saved his foot.

Turning over the command of the troops to General Chalmers, with instructions to complete the burial of the dead, collect the arms and other portable property, transfer, if possible, the Federal wounded to the first steamer that might be passing, and then follow, as soon as practicable, with the division and unwounded prisoners to Brownsville, Forrest[261] set out about sunset to return with his escort and staff to Jackson, Tennessee, encamping that night at a farm-house some six or seven miles eastward. Bell withdrew his brigade about one mile and a half east and encamped, while McCulloch's Brigade camped nearer the fort.

Wednesday, April 13th, 1864:

A detail was sent back to the fort to collect and remove the remaining arms and to finish burying the dead. They had been at work but a short time when a gunboat (the *Silver Cloud*) came up and began to shell them. A flag of truce and parley was hoisted, which being accepted by the Master of the *Silver Cloud*, Captain Ferguson, an arrangement soon resulted for a truce until five P.M. It was agreed that during that time the Federals might send parties ashore to visit all parts of the scene and look after their dead and wounded. During the day several transports came to the landing, and before the hour when the truce was to expire the wounded prisoners had all been tansferred to the cabin of the steamer *Platte Valley*, numbering about seventy, officers and men. Seven officers and two hundred and nineteen enlisted men (fifty-six negroes and one hundred and sixty-three whites), unwounded, were brought off as prisoners of war, which, with the wounded, make an aggregate of those who survived, exclusive of all who may have escaped (it was said that about twenty-five escaped in a skiff), two hundred and ninety-six, or a little over half of the garrison.

Having, several hours previous, put his main force in motion toward Brownsville, General Chalmers withdrew, about four P.M., with his staff and escort, in the same direction, and there remained at Fort Pillow none save the dead who had fallen in storming it, and the dead of the late garrison, victims, not of unlawful acts of war, as has been so virulently alleged and generally believed at the North, but of an insensate endeavor, as foolishly resolved as feebly executed, to hold a position naturally untenable and badly fortified; victims, we may add, of the imbecility and grievous mismanagement of those weak, incapable officers whom the fortunes of war

Confederate Lieutenant
B. A. High.

unhappily had placed over them. The two brigades camped some twelve miles east of the fort.

At Brownsville, that afternoon, the citizens of all classes—men, women, and children—received the Confederate General with tokens of deep-felt gratitude. The ladies of the vicinage, assembling at the courthouse, received him publicly, and testified their profound personal appreciation of his recent operations, by which they had been delivered from the apprehensions of further outrages, insults, and distressing annoyances from that pestilent band of ruffians and marauders which had been so thoroughly uprooted. The next day headquarters were re-established at Jackson, where Forrest remained until the 2nd of May.

COMMENTARIES FROM HANCOCK'S DIARY

1. In answer to an inquiry in reference to what command first entered the works at Fort Pillow, Colonel Barteau says:

> Colonel McCulloch and I met in the middle of the fort. He commanded the Second Missouri Cavalry as I did the Second Tennessee, and he came in from the extreme left next to the river as most of my regiment did from the extreme right next to the river. He and I talked the matter over, and we both concluded that we entered the fort just about the same time. I could not say for myself which was first, but Captain Farris thinks the Second Tennessee was first.

B. A. High and others agree with Captain Farris in thinking that the Second Tennessee was first to mount the parapet. As will be remembered, it was also the first to move up in close range of the fort. B. A. High was among the first to mount the works. Another man (whose name I have not been able to learn), in attempting to ascend rather in advance of High, was shot, and rolled back into the ditch a corpse, while High succeeded in going to the top, and captured a cannoneer, whose gun he soon after turned upon the Federal gunboat, as previously mentioned. Several of Company C were close after High. Among the number was J. C. McAdoo, who was long enough to jump into the ditch but too short to leap out until Colonel Bell came to his assistance.

In the manuscript notes of Colonel Barteau (which I have before me) I find the following:

> In this action the courage and self-reliance of the troops were particularly exhibited, and I think a satisfactory proof given to the commanding General that he could rely on his men in any emergency.
>
> Among my own soldiers who particularly distinguished themselves that day was Perry Marks, private of Company D, one of the first men on the fort, and also Lieutenant A. H. French, who was foremost with his men over the works, and Captain W. A. DeBow, who was in command of the regiment a part of the day.[262]
>
> 2. A flag of truce was sent in demanding the surrender. The answer received was one of defiance and insult, for the same reply that was given to General Forrest seemed to be the one heralded from the negroes on the works to our men on the outside. "If you want the fort come and take it," and "Damn you, what are you here for?"
>
> These were the taunts thrown out to our men who were during the truce in speaking distance. Moreover, several shots were fired during the truce at our men, who did not return them. No sooner had the flag retired than a defiant shout went up from the fort, and an active fire commenced. Our men, as by one impulse, seem to have determined they would take the fort, and that too independently of officers or orders, and had no command been given to "charge." I verily believe that after the insults given them during the truce they would have taken the fort by storm any way.
>
> 3. The troops in the fort had evidently been made drunk,

for those we took were more or less intoxicated, and we found barrels of whisky and ale and bottles of brandy open, and tin cups in the barrels out of which they had been drinking.

We also found water-buckets sitting around n the fort with whisky and dippers in them, which showed very clearly that the whisky had been thus passed around to the Federal troops.

The following, from the *Detroit Free Press* of December 1ˢᵗ, 1884, explains itself:

To the Editor of the *Detroit Free Press*:

Bartlett, Tenn.: — In the account given by "M Quad" of the Confederate capture of Fort Pillow he speaks of "Barton's Regiment." There was no such regiment in Forrest's Cavalry, but it was Barteau's Regiment, the Second Tennessee Cavalry, and as Colonel Barteau is still living, and is a convenient witness to all the particulars of that affair, I have taken the liberty to ask of him an expression upon "M Quad's" account of it.

Admitting "M Quad's" article to be an exceedingly forcible and succinct statement and a vivid description of the investment, assault, and capture of Fort Pillow in its general view, he yet differs from "M Quad" in his view of some features of the case.

Colonel Barteau says: "For days before the capture of Fort Pillow citizens fleeing to us from its vicinity brought doleful tales of outrages committed by the Federal forces in that stronghold. The helpless families of some of our soldiers had been victims of their raiding parties. A strong feeling prevailed in favor of capturing the fort, but it was not expected to be done without fighting and loss of life. If the commander of that garrison was taken by surprise it was gross negligence on his part; we surely did not expect to surprise him. But it seems that the Federals believed we would never storm their works, and this was their idea even up to the very moment of the assault, for during the truce, when our lines were in close speaking distance, a position we had gained by several hours' hard fighting, the negroes of the fort called to us with opprobrious names and dared us to the attempt. We did not move our position during the truce. We had gained it not without sacrifice; it was all we wanted then, for it was what we knew Forrest must have before he could be in a position to demand a surrender.

"It was the plain duty of the Federal commander, in view of the situation, to yield to the demand and thus save human life.

But he did not, and his men did not at all believe evidently that we would make the assault, and now foolhardy and unwise as they had been, when they saw us making for the ditch and climbing the parapet they were totally confounded with surprise.

"Nor did they surrender. They made a wild, crazy, scattering fight. They acted like a crowd of drunken men. They would at one moment yield and throw down their guns, and then would rush again to arms, seize their guns and renew the fire. If one squad was left as prisoners . . . it was soon discovered that they could not be trusted as having surrendered, for taking the first opportunity they would break loose again and engage in the contest. Some of our men were killed by [Union] negroes who had once surrendered.

"They would not, or at least did not, take down their flag. I ordered this done myself by my own men in order to stop the fight. If barbarities were committed, as 'M Quad' says, after the flag was taken down, it must have been under the circumstances of the contest as just stated. General Forrest came into the fort about this time, and all agree that he did not sanction them, nor could they have taken place in his presence. . . .

"I saw McCulloch, and we conversed about the affair the same evening after the capture. He was earnest in his expressions of the good conduct, forbearance, and obedience of his men after the foolhardy and strange manner in which the Federals had acted, causing unnecessary sacrifice of life.

"The third day after the surrender all the [Union] prisoners were placed in my charge, and I was ordered to take them from Sommerville with my regiment to Tupelo. On the way, which was several days' march, they freely expressed themselves as to the conduct of many of their white officers, and many of them admitted with expressions of condemnation the great error into which they had been led as to the defense of the fort, their drunkenness and folly of conduct, putting the blame upon their [Union] officers."

Colonel Barteau thinks that true history should place the blame upon the Federal side and not the Confederate. — John F. Cochran.[263]

NOTES

1. See Jones, TDMV, pp. 144, 200-201, 273.
2. See Seabrook, TAHSR, passim. See also, Pollard, LC, p. 178; J. H. Franklin, pp. 101, 111, 130, 149; Nicolay and Hay, ALCW, Vol. 1, p. 627.
3. See e.g., Seabrook, TQJD, pp. 30, 38, 76.
4. Seabrook, EYWTATCWIW, p. 13.
5. Wilson, pp. 70-71.
6. Brown, p. 235.
7. For more on these topics, see Seabrook, *Everything You Were Taught About American Slavery is Wrong, Ask a Southerner!*, passim.
8. Alexander, pp. 297-298.
9. Coburn, p. 44.
10. Hancock, p. 365.
11. Nicolay and Hay, ALCW, Vol. 2, pp. 513-514.
12. Jordan and Pryor, p. 448.
13. Denney, p. 392.
14. *Ohio Archaeological and Historical Quarterly*, Vol. 48, 1939, p. 40.
15. Mathes, p. 231.
16. Fort Pillow, built by the Confederacy in 1861 to aid in defending the water routes to Memphis, was taken over by the Yankees in 1862. Wills, pp. 179-180.
17. E. M. Thomas, p. 275.
18. J. Davis, Vol. 2, pp. 545-546.
19. ORA, Ser. 1, Vol. 32, Pt. 1, p. 596. See also Jordan and Pryor, p. 431.
20. Even Yankee officers, such as Captain Lewis M. Hosea, noted that Forrest was always extremely kind when it came to prisoners and the wounded. Gragg, p. 201.
21. Jordan and Pryor, p. 440.
22. See Long and Long, p. 484.
23. Henry ATSF, p. 157.
24. ORA, Ser. 1, Vol. 39, Pt. 1, p. 229. Among the "dastardly Yankee reporters" Forrest alludes to were those who worked for pro-Union Southern newspapers, such as the scallywag-run Memphis *Bulletin*, which helped nurture the "Fort Pillow Massacre" myth in a series of pro-North articles that began on April 13, 1864. Henry, FWMF, p. 266.
25. General Taylor goes on to say: "After the war I frequently met General Forrest, and received many evidences of attachment from him. He has passed away within a month, to the regret of all who knew him. In the States of Alabama, Mississippi, and Tennessee, to generations yet unborn, his name will be a 'household word.'" Taylor, pp. 200-201.
26. Hurst, p. 321.
27. Browning, p. 101.
28. Wills, p. 348.
29. Sheppard, pp. 294-296.
30. For the full story see Lytle, pp. 378-380.

31. Ashdown and Caudill, pp. 82-83. Comparing Forrest to Adolf Hitler is the height of irony, of course, for it was not Forrest who was similar to Hitler, it was Lincoln. Both men were socialistic racist dictators who used violence to try and destroy the ideas of states' rights and state sovereignty in their respective countries. Indeed, so enamored was Hitler of Lincoln (not Forrest) that he lovingly referenced Lincoln's tyrannical ideas in his book *Mein Kampf.* See Hitler, Vol. 2, pp. 830-831. Finally, Forrest was a political conservative, the opposite of a socialist. Hitler was the leader of the Nazis, or the National *Socialist* German Workers' Party, as it was more properly known. The phrase "New Deal," a series of economic reform programs instigated during Franklin D. Roosevelt's socialistic administration, was actually borrowed from the socialistic Lincoln administration, when it was coined to describe "Honest Abe's" progressive domestic policies. Seabrook, AL, pp. 491-492. For a detailed comparison between Lincoln and Hitler, see Seabrook, CCF, pp. 287-292.

32. Foote, Vol. 3, p. 111.

33. Mathes, p. 225.

34. Faust, s.v. "Fort Pillow, Tenn., Battle of."

35. Henry, FWMF, p. 259.

36. Jordan and Pryor, p. 444.

37. Current, TC, s.v. "African Americans in the Confederacy."

38. See e.g., Quarles, pp. 204-205; ORA, Ser. 3, Vol. 3, pp. 1126-1128.

39. Cornish, pp. 87, 269.

40. Lincoln also denied black Union soldiers pensions, bounties, and bonuses, all which were provided to white Union soldiers. See e.g., Leech, p. 312; Current, TC, s.v. "African Americans in the Confederacy."

41. Wyeth, LGNBF, p. 375.

42. Eaton, HSC, p. 264; Wyeth, LGNBF, p. 375.

43. Jordan and Pryor, p. 446.

44. My note: Forrest did not actually arrive until sometime between 9:00 and 11:00 AM—depending on the source—at which time he took over command from General James R. Chalmers.

45. ORA, Ser. 1, Vol. 32, Pt. 1, p. 559.

46. Jordan and Pryor, p. 446.

47. *Blackwood Magazine*, February 1867, p. 187.

48. Lytle, p. 279.

49. Cartmell, p. 146.

50. Mathes, p. 224.

51. Wyeth, LGNBF, p. 349.

52. Sheppard, p. 169; Mathes, p. 221.

53. Jordan and Pryor, pp. 449, 450.

54. Ashdown and Caudill, p. 83.

55. Jordan and Pryor, pp. 445-446.

56. Henry, FWMF, p. 266.

57. Lytle, p. 279.

58. Mathes, p. 227.

59. Pollard, SHW, Vol. 2, p. 260; Wyeth, LGNBF, pp. 348-349.

60. Eaton, HSC, p. 264.

61. Jordan and Pryor, pp. 434-440.
62. A. Ward, pp. 68, 157-158.
63. Mathes, p. 227.
64. Wyeth, LGNBF, pp. 334-337.
65. Wills, p. 185.
66. Browning, pp. 54-56; Jordan and Pryor, pp. 437-438.
67. Eaton, HSC, p. 264.
68. Foote, Vol. 3, p. 112.
69. "Lieutenant-General N. B. Forrest: Lord Wolseley's Estimate of the Man and the Soldier," *Southern Historical Society Papers*, Vol. 20, 1892, p. 331 (original from the New Orleans *Picayune*, April 10, 1892).
70. Mathes, p. 225.
71. Wyeth, LGNBF, p. 356.
72. Jordan and Pryor, p. 439. In discussing Fort Pillow pro-North writers only focus on the Union losses. It is important to remember, however, that Forrest also suffered loss of life in his own command: by some counts at least fourteen of his officers and men died, while eighty-six were wounded. Jordan and Pryor, p. 441.
73. Jordan and Pryor, p. 444.
74. Mathes, p. 219; Browning, p. 52.
75. Mathes, pp. 220, 223.
76. Sheppard, p. 169.
77. Jordan and Pryor, p. 440.
78. Wyeth, LGBNF, p. 383.
79. Ashdown and Caudill, p. 36.
80. Henry, FWMF, p. 265.
81. Wills, pp. 185, 186.
82. Jordan and Pryor, p. 432; Sheppard, p. 167; Wills, pp. 184, 185, 186.
83. Mathes, p. 227.
84. Jordan and Pryor, pp. 434, 435.
85. Wyeth, LGNBF, p. 348.
86. Lytle, p. 278.
87. Jordan and Pryor, pp. 422, 424.
88. Lytle, p. 277.
89. Mathes, pp. 214-215, 228.
90. Bradley, pp. 11-12.
91. Nicolay and Hay, ALCW, Vol. 2, p. 288.
92. Wyeth, LGNBF, p. 366.
93. ORA, Ser. 1, Vol. 39, Pt. 1, p. 521.
94. Ashdown and Caudill, p. 42.
95. Morton, p. 191.
96. Mathes, p. 214.
97. Ashdown and Caudill, p. 83.
98. Jordan and Pryor, pp. 422-423.
99. ORA, Ser. 1, Vol. 32, Pt. 1, p. 609.
100. Mathes, p. 215.

101. Pollard, SHW, Vol. 2, p. 261.

102. Smith, p. 320.

103. Jordan and Pryor, pp. 489-492.

104. Henry ATSF, p. 158.

105. A. Ward, pp. 78, 161.

106. Seabrook, EYWTAASIW, passim; J. C. Perry, pp. 218, 223.

107. Lytle, p. 279. Many of the black Union soldiers at Fort Pillow were recently freed slaves who were, no doubt, in a celebratory mood that day; hence the over-consumption of alcohol.

108. Jordan and Pryor, pp. 439-440.

109. Mathes, p. 227.

110. Wyeth, LGNBF, p. 350.

111. Wyeth, LGNBF, pp. 351, 386.

112. Wyeth, LGNBF, pp. 349-351.

113. In northeastern Mississippi, for example, Smith and his men robbed and pillaged the people, laying waste the country to the point where it was described as "almost a desert." Lytle, p. 289.

114. ORA, Ser. 1, Vol. 32, Pt. 3, pp. 664-665.

115. ORA, Ser. 1, Vol. 32, Pt. 1, pp. 118-119.

116. Wills, p. 173.

117. ORA, Ser. 1, Vol. 32, Pt. 1, p. 119.

118. Jordan and Pryor, pp. 549-552.

119. Lytle, pp. 148-149. For more on the three Battles of Franklin, see Seabrook, EOTBOF, passim.

120. Wills, p. 108.

121. Jordan and Pryor, p. 247.

122. Morton, p. 88.

123. Wyeth, LGNBF, p. 184.

124. Mathes, p. 107; Sheppard, pp. 99-100.

125. ORA, Ser. 1, Vol. 39, Pt. 3, p. 494.

126. Sherman, Vol. 2, p. 194.

127. Watts, s.v. "galvanized Yankee"; Faust, s.v. "Galvanized Yankees."

128. Wills, p. 192.

129. Mathes, p. 215.

130. See e.g., Wyeth, LGNBF, p. 589.

131. Wyeth, LGNBF, p. 589.

132. Henry, ATSF, pp. 126, 151.

133. Wyeth, LGNBF, p. 368-369.

134. Wyeth, LGNBF, pp. 335-337.

135. Wyeth, LGNBF, p. 354.

136. Jordan and Pryor, pp. 432-433.

137. Jordan and Pryor, pp. 433, 437-438.

138. Wyeth, LGNBF, pp. 344-345.

139. Wyeth, LGNBF, p. 385. Actually, it was black U.S. soldiers who had taken an government oath to "give no quarter" to Forrest. Jordan and Pryor, pp. 482, 485-487, 519.

140. Wyeth, LGNBF, pp. 345-346.
141. Browning, p. 53.
142. Jordan and Pryor, p. 442.
143. Jordan and Pryor, pp. 437-439.
144. Wyeth, LGNBF, p. 355.
145. *Southern Historical Society Papers*, Vol. 7, 1879, p. 439.
146. Wyeth, LGNBF, p. 381.
147. Wyeth, LGNBF, p. 356.
148. Jordan and Pryor, p. 442.
149. Mathes, p. 225.
150. ORA, Ser. 1, Vol. 32, Pt. 2, p. 664.
151. Jordan and Pryor, p. 443.
152. Wyeth, LGNBF, p. 358.
153. Jordan and Pryor, p. 443.
154. Mathes, p. 226.
155. Jordan and Pryor, p. 450.
156. Wyeth, LGNBF, p. 379; Jordan and Pryor, p. 443.
157. Lytle, p. 280.
158. Jordan and Pryor, pp. 440-441.
159. After arriving at Brownsville Forrest was met by the local townswomen, who thanked him for shutting down Fort Pillow. As a gift of appreciation they had their sewing thimbles melted down, and from them were cast a pair of silver spurs for the General. Lytle, p. 280.
160. Mathes, p. 228.
161. Jordan and Pryor, p. 455.
162. Jordan and Pryor, p. 455.
163. Wyeth, LGNBF, p. 361.
164. Mathes, p. 226.
165. Wyeth, LGNBF, p. 384.
166. Jordan and Pryor, pp. 442-443.
167. Wyeth, LGNBF, p. 379.
168. Wyeth, LGNBF, pp. 357-358.
169. ORA, Ser. 1, Vol. 32, Pt. 3, p. 664.
170. Mathes, pp. 228, 229.
171. Wyeth, LGNBF, p. 381.
172. Sheppard, pp. 171-172.
173. ORA, Ser. 1, Vol. 32, Pt. 1, p. 561.
174. Wyeth, LGNBF, pp. 345-346.
175. Wyeth, LGNBF, p. 346.
176. ORA, Ser. 1, Vol. 32, Pt. 1, pp. 572-574.
177. ORA, Ser. 1, Vol. 32, Pt. 1, p. 610.
178. Henry, FWMF, p. 259.
179. Wyeth, LGNBF, p. 362.
180. U. S. Grant, Vol. 1, p. 138.
181. Wyeth, LGNBF, p. 362.

182. See e.g., Andrew Ward's polemic and caustic anti-South title: *River Run Red: The Fort Pillow Massacre in the American Civil War.*

183. Faust, s.v. "Fort Pillow, Tenn., Battle of."

184. Foote, Vol. 3, p. 112.

185. J. M. McPherson, BCF, p. 794.

186. Woodward, p. 596.

187. ORA, Ser. 1, Vol. 32, Pt. 3, p. 366.

188. Wyeth, LGNBF, p. 382.

189. Woodward, p. 596; J. M. McPherson, BCF, p. 794; Foote, Vol. 3, p. 112; Wyeth, LGNBF, p. 382.

190. Henry, FWMF, p. 268.

191. A. Ward, p. 323. For more on Lincoln's racist beliefs and policies see my books, ALSV, passim; TUAL, passim; L, passim; and TGI, passim.

192. Sherman, Vol. 2, pp. 12-13.

193. Wyeth, LGNBF, pp. 346-387.

194. Wills, pp. 189-190.

195. *Reports of Committees of the Senate of the United States*, p. 40.

196. ORA, Ser. 1, Vol. 32, Pt. 1, p. 558.

197. Wyeth, LGNBF, p. 390.

198. Morton, p. 191; Wills, pp. 187-188.

199. Encyc. Brit., s.v. "Forrest, Nathan Bedford."

200. Wyeth, LGNBF, pp. 386-387.

201. Forrest lost three horses at Fort Pillow, illustrating the severity of the battle. Wyeth, LGNBF, pp. 342, 606; Jordan and Pryor, p. 429.

202. Mathes, p. 361.

203. ORA, Ser. 1, Vol. 32, Pt. 1, p. 591.

204. For more on Forrest's racial views and beliefs see Seabrook, ARB, passim; Seabrook, TQNBF; passim; Seabrook, F99R, passim; Seabrook, GEHB, passim; Seabrook, NBF, passim; Seabrook, SSG, passim; and Seabrook, NBFKKK, passim.

205. ORA, Ser. 1, Vol. 32, Pt. 1, pp. 613-617.

206. ORA, Ser. 1, Vol. 32, Pt. 1, p. 617.

207. ORA, Ser. 1, Vol. 32, Pt. 1, p. 617.

208. ORA, Ser. 1, Vol. 32, Pt. 1, p. 617.

209. ORA, Ser. 1, Vol. 32, Pt. 1, pp. 617-618.

210. ORA, Ser. 1, Vol. 32, Pt. 1, p. 618.

211. ORA, Ser. 1, Vol. 32, Pt. 1, p. 619.

212. ORA, Ser. 1, Vol. 32, Pt. 1, p. 619.

213. Warner, GB, s.v. "Cadwallader Colden Washburn."

214. ORA, Ser. 1, Vol. 32, Pt. 1, pp. 590-591.

215. ORA, Ser. 1, Vol. 32, Pt. 1, pp. 591-593.

216. Johnson and Buell, Vol. 4, p. 418.

217. Mathes, p. 227.

218. Jordan and Pryor, p. 446.

219. Wyeth, LGNBF, p. 367.

220. Wyeth, LGNBF, p. 427.

221. Browning, p. 56.
222. Browning, pp. 56-58.
223. Sheppard, p. 171.
224. Mathes, pp. 229-231.
225. Cornish, p. 173.
226. Sheppard, p. 172.
227. Lytle, p. 280.
228. *Reports of Committees of the Senate of the United States*, p. 30.
229. See e.g., Wyeth, LGNBF, pp. 346-387.
230. Jordan and Pryor, pp. 452-453. See also the *Memphis Commercial Appeal*, May 30, 1901; May 17, 1905; May 7, 1988.
231. Henry, FWMF, p. 260.
232. *Reports of Committees of the Senate of the United States*, p. 15.
233. *Reports of Committees of the Senate of the United States*, p. 27.
234. ORA, Ser. 1, Vol. 32, Pt. 1, p. 596; Jordan and Pryor, p. 431.
235. Jordan and Pryor, p. 431.
236. See Browning, p. 58.
237. See e.g., Nicolay and Hay, ALCW, Vol. 1, pp. 289, 370, 457, 458, 469, 539; Basler, ALSW, pp. 400, 402, 403-404; Stern, pp. 492-493; Holzer, pp. 189, 251.
238. See e.g., Nicolay and Hay, CWAL, Vol. 11, pp. 105-106; Nicolay and Hay, ALCW, Vol. 1, p. 483; Holzer, pp. 22-23, 67, 318, 361.
239. See e.g., Barrow, Segars, and Rosenburg, BC, p. 4; Mullen, p. 31; L. Johnson, p. 134; *Charlotte Daily Bulletin*, November 13, 1862; *The Liberator*, May 22, 1863; Leech, p. 312; Current, TC, s.v. "African Americans in the Confederacy"; Quarles, pp. 64, 204-205; Faust, s.v. "black soldiers"; Simmons, s.v. "Negro troops"; Smith, p. 308; Adams, p. 134; Henderson, Vol. 2, p. 411; Cartmell, pp. 144, 145; Alotta, pp. 26-28.
240. Seabrook, TUAL, p. 91.
241. *Douglass' Monthly*, March 1863, Vol. 5, p. 802. My paraphrasal.
242. Hurst, pp. 382, 414.
243. Davison and Foxx, p. 424. My paraphrasal.
244. Witherspoon is a relation of my cousin, Louisiana native and Oscar-winning actress Reese Witherspoon. One of Reese's ancestors, Scotsman John Witherspoon, was a signatory of the Declaration of Independence, a document that was near and dear to traditional Southerners like Forrest.
245. Henry, ATSF, p. 125. My paraphrasal.
246. Jordan and Pryor, p. 453.
247. Pollard, LC, p. 499.
248. Sachsman, Rushing, and Morris, p. 325; Davison and Foxx, p. 424. My paraphrasal.
249. Cimprich, p. 83.
250. Bedwell, p. 66.
251. Wyeth, LGNBF, pp. 370-371.
252. *Confederate Veteran*, November 1895, Vol. 3, No. 11, pp. 322-326.
253. Hancock's note: "The writer heard Forrest remark as he passed: 'There are not many—we must take them.'"

254. Hancock's note: "I do not know why Captain Marshall, the commander of the gunboat, ceased firing when he could have used his guns with such telling effect upon our regiment, unless it was because he was scarce of ammunition or afraid to open his port-holes, fearing we would kill his gunners."

255. Hancock's note: "After some discussion among the officers present it was agreed by both Forrest and Chalmers, 'that if the port was surrendered the whole garrison, white and black, should be treated as prisoners of war.'"

256. Hancock's note: "These were the *Olive Branch*, with General Shipley [Shepley] and troops on board, the *Hope*, and the *M. R. Cheek*."

257. Hancock's note: "Doak Carr (Company D, Second Tennessee) took down the Federal flag."

258. Hancock's note: "So well was one of these guns handled by B. A. High (who was afterward made Orderly Sergeant, Company G, Second Tennessee) that Forrest offered to promote him to the rank of Captain and allow him to go with the captured guns to Mobile, Alabama. He declined to take the command of the battery from the fact that he was not willing to leave his comrades. He would have accepted if Forrest had kept the battery with his own command."

259. Hancock's note: "Captain O. B. Farris (Company K, Second Tennessee) superintended the burial of the dead."

260. Hancock's note: "Major Bradford . . . was, several days afterward, recaptured in disguise. At first he affected to be a conscript, but being recognized was remanded to custody as a prisoner of war. He was then sent in charge of a party—a subaltern and some five or six men—to Brownsville. On the way he again attempted to escape, soon after which one of the men shot him. It was an act in which no officer was concerned, mainly due, we are satisfied, after the most rigid inquiry, to private vengeance for well authenticated outrages committed by Bradford and his band upon the defenseless families of the men of Forrest's Cavalry."

261. Hancock's note: "Just after the firing had ceased (about three P.M.), and while standing inside the fort, the writer heard Forrest say, pointing to the eminence from which he had caused the signal for the assault to be given: 'When from my position on that hill I saw my men pouring over these breastworks, it seemed'—now placing his right-hand upon his left breast—'that my heart would burst within me.' 'Men,' continued he, 'if you will do as I say I will always lead you to victory. I have taken every place that the Federals occupied in West Tennessee and North Mississippi except Memphis, and if they don't mind I'll have that place too in less than six weeks. They killed two horses from under me to-day'—a third was wounded—'and knocked me to my knees a time or two, so I thought by damned they were going to get me any way."

262. Hancock's note: "Our Lieutenant-Colonel (Morton) was absent on account of a wound received at Paducah."

263. Hancock, pp. 352-369.

BIBLIOGRAPHY

Adams, Charles. *When in the Course of Human Events: Arguing the Case for Southern Secession*. Lanham, MD: Rowman and Littlefield, 2000.

Alexander, William T. *History of the Colored Race in America*. 1887. Kansas City, MO: Palmetto Publishing Co., 1899 ed.

Alotta, Robert I. *Civil War Justice: Union Army Executions Under Lincoln*. Shippensburg, PA: White Mane, 1989.

Ashdown, Paul, and Edward Caudill. *The Myth of Nathan Bedford Forrest*. 2005. Lanham, MD: Rowman and Littlefield, 2006 ed.

Barrow, Charles Kelly, J. H. Segars, and R. B. Rosenburg (eds.). *Black Confederates*. 1995. Gretna, LA: Pelican Publishing Co., 2001 ed.

———. *Forgotten Confederates: An Anthology About Black Southerners*. Saint Petersburg, FL: Southern Heritage Press, 1997.

Basler, Roy Prentice (ed.). *Abraham Lincoln: His Speeches and Writings*. 1946. New York, NY: Da Capo Press, 2001 ed.

——— (ed.). *The Collected Works of Abraham Lincoln*. 9 vols. New Brunswick, NJ: Rutgers University Press, 1953.

Bedwell, Randall (ed.). *May I Quote You, General Forrest? Observations and Utterances from the South's Great Generals*. Nashville, TN: Cumberland House, 1997.

Bradley, Michael R. *Nathan Bedford Forrest's Escort and Staff*. Gretna, LA: Pelican Publishing Co., 2006.

Browder, Earl. *Lincoln and the Communists*. New York, NY: Workers Library Publishers, Inc., 1936.

Brown, William Wells. *The Negro in the American Rebellion: His Heroism and His Fidelity*. Boston, MA: Lee and Shephard, 1867.

Browning, Robert, M., Jr. *Forrest: The Confederacy's Relentless Warrior*. Dulles, VA: Brassey's, Inc., 2004.

Cartmell, Donald. *Civil War 101*. New York, NY: Gramercy, 2001.

Cimprich, John. *Fort Pillow, a Civil War Massacre, and Public Memory*. Baton Rouge, LA: Louisiana State University Press, 2005.

Coburn, Frederick William. *Moses Greeley Parker, M.D.* Lowell, MA: self-published, 1921.

Cornish, Dudley Taylor. *The Sable Arm: Black Troops in the Union Army, 1861-1865*. 1956. Lawrence, KS: University Press of Kansas, 1987 ed.

Current, Richard N. *The Lincoln Nobody Knows*. 1958. New York, NY: Hill and Wang, 1963 ed.

———. (ed.). *The Confederacy (Information Now Encyclopedia)*. 1993. New York, NY: Macmillan, 1998 ed.

Davis, Jefferson. *The Rise and Fall of the Confederate Government*. 2 vols. New York, NY: D. Appleton and Co., 1881.

Davison, Eddy W., and Daniel Foxx. *Nathan Bedford Forrest: In Search of the Enigma*.

Gretna, LA: Pelican Publishing Co., 2007.

Denney, Robert E. *The Civil War Years: A Day-by-Day Chronicle of the Life of a Nation.* 1992. New York, NY: Sterling Publishing Co., 1994 ed.

Eaton, Clement. *A History of the Southern Confederacy.* 1945. New York, NY: Free Press, 1966 ed.

——. *Jefferson Davis.* New York, NY: Free Press, 1977.

Encyclopedia Britannica: A New Survey of Human Knowledge. 1929. Chicago, IL: Encyclopedia Britannica, Inc., 1955 ed.

Faust, Patricia L. (ed.). *Historical Times Illustrated Encyclopedia of the Civil War.* New York, NY: Harper and Row, 1986.

Foote, Shelby. *The Civil War: A Narrative, Fort Sumter to Perryville, Vol. I.* 1958. New York, NY: Vintage, 1986, ed.

——. *The Civil War: A Narrative, Fredericksburg to Meridian, Vol. II.* 1963. New York, NY: Vintage, 1986, ed.

——. *The Civil War: A Narrative, Red River to Appomattox, Vol. III.* 1974. New York, NY: Vintage, 1986, ed.

Franklin, John Hope. *Reconstruction After the Civil War.* Chicago, IL: University of Chicago Press, 1961.

Gragg, Rod. *The Illustrated Confederate Reader: Extraordinary Eyewitness Accounts by the Civil War's Southern Soldiers and Civilians.* New York, NY: Gramercy Books, 1989.

Grant, Ulysses Simpson. *Personal Memoirs of U. S. Grant.* 2 vols. 1885-1886. New York, NY: Charles L. Webster and Co., 1886.

Hancock, Richard R. *Hancock's Diary: Or, A History of the Second Tennessee Confederate Cavalry.* 2 vols in 1. Nashville, TN: Brandon Printing Co., 1887.

Henderson, George Francis Robert. *Stonewall Jackson and the American Civil War.* 2 vols. London, UK: Longmans, Green, and Co., 1919.

Henry, Robert Selph. *The Story of the Confederacy.* 1931. New York, NY: Konecky and Konecky, 1999 ed.

——. (ed.). *As They Saw Forrest: Some Recollections and Comments of Contemporaries.* 1956. Wilmington, NC: Broadfoot Publishing Co., 1991 ed.

——. *First with the Most: Forrest.* New York, NY: Konecky and Konecky, 1992.

Hitler, Adolf. *Mein Kampf.* 2 vols. 1925, 1926. New York: NY: Reynal and Hitchcock, 1941 English translation ed.

Holzer, Harold (ed.). *The Lincoln-Douglas Debates: The First Complete, Unexpurgated Text.* 1993. Bronx, NY: Fordham University Press, 2004 ed.

Hurst, Jack. *Nathan Bedford Forrest: A Biography.* 1993. New York, NY: Vintage, 1994 ed.

Johnson, Ludwell H. *North Against South: The American Iliad, 1848-1877.* 1978. Columbia, SC: Foundation for American Education, 1993 ed.

Johnson, Robert Underwood, and Clarence Clough Buell (eds.). *Battles and Leaders of the Civil War.* 4 vols. 1884. New York, NY: The Century Co., 1888 ed.

Johnstone, Huger William. *Truth of War Conspiracy, 1861.* Idylwild, GA: H. W. Johnstone, 1921.

Jones, John William. *The Davis Memorial Volume; Or Our Dead President, Jefferson Davis and the World's Tribute to His Memory.* Richmond, VA: B. F. Johnson, 1889.

Jordan, Thomas, and John P. Pryor. *The Campaigns of General Nathan Bedford Forrest and of Forrest's Cavalry.* New Orleans, LA: Blelock and Co., 1868.

Leech, Margaret. *Reveille in Washington, 1860-1865.* 1941. Alexandria, VA: Time-Life Books, 1980 ed.

Long, E. B., and Barbara Long. *The Civil War Day By Day: An Almanac 1861-1865.* Cambridge, MA: Da Capo Press, 1971.

Lytle, Andrew Nelson. *Bedford Forrest and His Critter Company.* New York, NY: G. P. Putnam's Sons, 1931.

Mathes, Capt. J. Harvey. *General Forrest.* New York, NY: D. Appleton and Co., 1902.

McCarty, Burke (ed.). *Little Sermons In Socialism by Abraham Lincoln.* Chicago, IL: The Chicago Daily Socialist, 1910.

McPherson, Edward. *The Political History of the United States of America, During the Great Rebellion (From November 6, 1860, to July 4, 1864).* Washington, D.C.: Philp and Solomons, 1864.

——. *The Political History of the United States of America, During the Period of Reconstruction, (From April 15, 1865, to July 15, 1870,) Including a Classified Summary of the Legislation of the Thirty-ninth, Fortieth, and Forty-first Congresses.* Washington, D.C.: Solomons and Chapman, 1875.

McPherson, James M. *The Struggle for Equality: Abolitionists and the Negro in the Civil War and Reconstruction.* 1964. Princeton, NJ: Princeton University Press, 1992 ed.

——. *The Negro's Civil War: How American Negroes Felt and Acted During the War for the Union.* 1965. Chicago, IL: University of Illinois Press, 1982 ed.

——. *Battle Cry of Freedom: The Civil War Era.* Oxford, UK: Oxford University Press, 2003.

——. *The Atlas of the Civil War.* Philadelphia, PA: Courage Books, 2005.

McPherson, James M., and the staff of the *New York Times.* *The Most Fearful Ordeal: Original Coverage of the Civil War by Writers and Reporters of the New York Times.* New York, NY: St. Martin's Press, 2004.

McWhiney, Grady, and Judith Lee Hallock. *Braxton Bragg and Confederate Defeat.* 2 vols. Tuscaloosa, AL: University of Alabama Press, 1991.

McWhiney, Grady, and Perry D. Jamieson. *Attack and Die: Civil War Military Tactics and the Southern Heritage.* Tuscaloosa, AL: University of Alabama Press, 1982.

Morton, John Watson. *The Artillery of Nathan Bedford Forrest's Cavalry.* Nashville, TN: The M. E. Church, 1909.

Mullen, Robert W. *Blacks in America's Wars: The Shift in Attitudes from the Revolutionary War to Vietnam.* 1973. New York, NY: Pathfinder, 1991 ed.

Nicolay, John George, and John Hay (eds.). *Abraham Lincoln: Complete Works.* 12 vols. New York, NY: The Century Co., 1907.

ORA (full title: *The War of the Rebellion: A Compilation of the Official Records of the Union and Confederate Armies.* (Multiple volumes.) Washington, D.C.: Government Printing Office, 1880.

ORN (full title: *Official Records of the Union and Confederate Navies in the War of the Rebellion*). (Multiple volumes.) Washington, D.C.: Government Printing Office, 1894.

Perry, John C. *Myths and Realities of American Slavery: The True History of Slavery in America.* Shippenburg, PA: Burd Street Press, 2002.

Pollard, Edward A. *Southern History of the War.* 2 vols in 1. New York, NY: Charles B. Richardson, 1866.

——. *The Lost Cause.* 1867. Chicago, IL: E. B. Treat, 1890 ed.

——. *Lee and His Lieutenants: Comprising the Early Life, Public Services, and Campaigns of General Robert E. Lee and His Companions in Arms.* New York, NY: E. B. Treat, 1867.

——. *The Lost Cause Regained.* New York, NY: G. W. Carlton and Co., 1868.

——. *Life of Jefferson Davis, With a Secret History of the Southern Confederacy, Gathered "Behind the Scenes in Richmond."* Philadelphia, PA: National Publishing Co., 1869.

Quarles, Benjamin. *The Negro in the Civil War.* 1953. Cambridge, MA: Da Capo Press, 1988 ed.

Reports of Committees of the Senate of the United States (for the Thirty-eighth Congress). Washington, D.C.: Government Printing Office, 1864.

Report of the Joint Committee on Reconstruction (at the First Session, Thirty-ninth Congress). Washington, D.C.: Government Printing Office, 1866.

Report of the Joint Select Committee to Inquire into the Condition of Affairs in the Late Insurrectionary States. Washington, D.C.: Government Printing Office, 1872.

Reports of Committees of the Senate of the United States (for the Second Session of the Forty-second Congress). Washington, D.C.: Government Printing Office, 1872.

Sachsman, David B., S. Kittrell Rushing, and Roy Morris, Jr. (eds.). *Words at War: The Civil War and American Journalism.* West Lafayette, IN: Purdue University Press, 2008.

Seabrook, Lochlainn. *Nathan Bedford Forrest: Southern Hero, American Patriot.* 2007. Franklin, TN: Sea Raven Press, 2015 ed.

——. *Abraham Lincoln: The Southern View.* 2007. Franklin, TN: Sea Raven Press, 2013 ed.

——. *A Rebel Born: A Defense of Nathan Bedford Forrest.* 2010. Franklin, TN: Sea Raven Press, 2011 ed.

——. *A Rebel Born: The Screenplay.* Unpublished screenplay. Franklin, TN: Sea Raven Press.

——. *Everything You Were Taught About the Civil War is Wrong, Ask a Southerner!* 2010. Franklin, TN: Sea Raven Press, revised 2014 ed.

——. *The Quotable Jefferson Davis: Selections From the Writings and Speeches of the Confederacy's First President.* Franklin, TN: Sea Raven Press, 2011.

——. *Lincolnology: The Real Abraham Lincoln Revealed In His Own Words.* Franklin, TN:

Sea Raven Press, 2011.

——. *The Unquotable Abraham Lincoln: The President's Quotes They Don't Want You To Know!* Franklin, TN: Sea Raven Press, 2011.

——. *The Quotable Nathan Bedford Forrest: Selections From the Writings and Speeches of the Confederacy's Most Brilliant Cavalryman.* Franklin, TN: Sea Raven Press, 2012.

——. *Give 'Em Hell Boys! The Complete Military Correspondence of Nathan Bedford Forrest.* Franklin, TN: Sea Raven Press, 2012.

——. *The Great Impersonator: 99 Reasons to Dislike Abraham Lincoln.* Franklin, TN: Sea Raven Press, 2012.

——. *Forrest! 99 Reasons to Love Nathan Bedford Forrest.* Franklin, TN: Sea Raven Press, 2012.

——. *The Alexander H. Stephens Reader: Excerpts From the Works of a Confederate Founding Father.* Franklin, TN: Sea Raven Press, 2013.

——. *Saddle, Sword, and Gun: A Biography of Nathan Bedford Forrest For Teens.* Franklin, TN: Sea Raven Press, 2013.

——. *Everything You Were Taught About American Slavery War is Wrong, Ask a Southerner!* Franklin, TN: Sea Raven Press, 2015.

——. *Confederacy 101: Amazing Facts You Never Knew About America's Oldest Political Tradition.* Franklin, TN: Sea Raven Press, 2015.

——. *The Great Yankee Coverup: What the North Doesn't Want You to Know About Lincoln's War!* Franklin, TN: Sea Raven Press, 2015.

——. *Confederate Flag Facts: What Every American Should Know About Dixie's Southern Cross.* Franklin, TN: Sea Raven Press, 2015.

——. *Nathan Bedford Forrest and the Ku Klux Klan: Yankee Myth, Confederate Fact.* Franklin, TN: Sea Raven Press, 2015.

Sherman, William Tecumseh. *Memoirs of General William T. Sherman.* 2 vols. 1875. New York, NY: D. Appleton and Co., 1891 ed.

Smith, Page. *Trial by Fire: A People's History of the Civil War and Reconstruction.* New York, NY: McGraw-Hill, 1982.

Stern, Philip Van Doren (ed.). *The Life and Writings of Abraham Lincoln.* 1940. New York, NY: Modern Library, 2000 ed.

Taylor, Richard. *Destruction and Reconstruction: Personal Experiences of the Late War in the United States.* New York, NY: D. Appleton, 1879.

Thomas, Emory M. *The Confederate Nation: 1861-1865.* New York, NY: Harper and Row, 1979.

Ward, Andrew. *River Run Red: The Fort Pillow Massacre in the American Civil War.* New York, NY: Viking, 2005.

Warner, Ezra J. *Generals in Gray: Lives of the Confederate Commanders.* 1959. Baton Rouge, LA: Louisiana State University Press, 1989 ed.

——. *Generals in Blue: Lives of the Union Commanders.* 1964. Baton Rouge, LA: Louisiana State University Press, 2006 ed.

Watts, Peter. *A Dictionary of the Old West.* 1977. New York, NY: Promontory Press, 1987 ed.

Wills, Brian Steel. *The Confederacy's Greatest Cavalryman: Nathan Bedford Forrest.* Lawrence, KS: University Press of Kansas, 1992.

Wilson, Thomas L. *Sufferings Endured For a Free Government: A History of the Cruelties and Atrocities of the Rebellion.* 1864. Philadelphia, PA: King and Baird, 1865 ed.

Woodward, William E. *Meet General Grant.* 1928. New York, NY: Liveright Publishing, 1946 ed.

Wyeth, John Allan. *Life of General Nathan Bedford Forrest.* New York, NY: Harper and Brothers, 1899.

——. *That Devil Forrest* (redacted modern version of Wyeth's *Life of General Nathan Bedford Forrest*). 1959. Baton Rouge, LA: Louisiana State University Press, 1989 ed.

Forrest as a Memphis alderman in 1850.

INDEX

General Nathan Bedford Forrest's high morals, sterling character, and stainless integrity were attested to by all who knew him, including women, free blacks, his former "slaves," and even many of his onetime Yankee foes. Forrest was later scrutinized before a biased U.S. government committee investigating the Battle of Fort Pillow. Following an exhaustive interrogation, the panel cleared him, finding the General innocent of any and all crimes associated with the conflict. The truth has now been firmly and permanently established, and the South is closing the book on this unfortunate chapter of American history for the last time—a chapter, it must be acknowledged, for which the North itself must bear full responsibility. From this point on further debate over, as well as slander against, the Confederate action at Henning can be nothing else but the product of ignorance, bias, and anti-South malice.

MEET THE AUTHOR

OCHLAINN SEABROOK, winner of the prestigious Jefferson Davis Historical Gold Medal for his "masterpiece," *A Rebel Born: A Defense of Nathan Bedford Forrest*, is an unreconstructed Southern historian, award-winning author, Civil War scholar, and traditional Southern Agrarian of Scottish, English, Irish, Dutch, Welsh, German, and Italian extraction. An encyclopedist, lexicographer, musician, artist, graphic designer, genealogist, and photographer, as well as an award-winning poet, songwriter, and screenwriter, he has a 40 year background in historical nonfiction writing and is a member of the Sons of Confederate Veterans, the Civil War Trust, and the National Grange.

Due to similarities in their writing styles, ideas, and literary works, Seabrook is often referred to as the "new Shelby Foote," the "Southern Joseph Campbell," and the "American Robert Graves" (his English cousin).

The grandson of an Appalachian coal-mining family, Seabrook is a seventh-generation Kentuckian, co-chair of the Jent/Gent Family Committee (Kentucky), founder and director of the Blakeney Family Tree Project, and a board member of the Friends of Colonel Benjamin E. Caudill.

COPYRIGHT ©
SEA RAVEN PRESS

Lochlainn Seabrook, award-winning Civil War scholar and unreconstructed Southern historian, is America's most popular and prolific pro-South author.

Seabrook's literary works have been endorsed by leading authorities, museum curators, award-winning historians, bestselling authors, celebrities, noted scientists, well respected educators, TV show hosts and producers, renowned military artists, esteemed Southern organizations, and distinguished academicians from around the world.

Seabrook has authored over 45 popular adult books on the American Civil War, American and international slavery, the U.S. Confederacy (1781), the Southern Confederacy (1861), religion, theology and thealogy, Jesus, the Bible, the Apocrypha, the Law of Attraction, alternative health, spirituality, ghost stories, the paranormal, ufology, social issues, and cross-cultural studies of the family and marriage. His Confederate biographies, pro-South studies, genealogical monographs, family histories, military encyclopedias, self-help guides, and etymological dictionaries have received wide acclaim.

Seabrook's eight children's books include a Southern guide to the Civil War, a biography of Nathan Bedford Forrest, a dictionary of religion and myth, a rewriting of the King Arthur legend (which reinstates the original pre-Christian motifs), two bedtime stories for preschoolers, a naturalist's guidebook to owls, a worldwide look at the family, and an examination of the Near-Death Experience.

Of blue-blooded Southern stock through his Kentucky, Tennessee, Virginia, West Virginia, and North Carolina ancestors, he is a direct descendant of European royalty via his 6th great-grandfather, the Earl of Oxford, after which London's famous Harley Street is named. Among his celebrated male Celtic ancestors is Robert the Bruce, King of Scotland, Seabrook's 22nd great-grandfather. The 21st great-grandson of Edward I "Longshanks" Plantagenet), King of England, Seabrook is a thirteenth-generation Southerner through his descent from the colonists of Jamestown, Virginia (1607).

The 2nd, 3rd, and 4th great-grandson of dozens of Confederate soldiers, one of his closest connections to Lincoln's War is through his 3rd great-grandfather, Elias Jent, Sr., who fought for the

Confederacy in the Thirteenth Cavalry Kentucky under Seabrook's 2nd cousin, Colonel Benjamin E. Caudill. The Thirteenth, also known as "Caudill's Army," fought in numerous conflicts, including the Battles of Saltville, Gladsville, Mill Cliff, Poor Fork, Whitesburg, and Leatherwood.

Seabrook is a direct descendant of the families of Alexander H. Stephens, John Singleton Mosby, William Giles Harding, and Edmund Winchester Rucker, and is related to the following Confederates and other 18th- and 19th-Century luminaries: Robert E. Lee, Stephen Dill Lee, Stonewall Jackson, Nathan Bedford Forrest, James Longstreet, John Hunt Morgan, Jeb Stuart, Pierre G. T. Beauregard (approved the Confederate Battle Flag design), George W. Gordon, John Bell Hood, Alexander Peter Stewart, Arthur M. Manigault, Joseph Manigault, Charles Scott Venable, Thornton A. Washington, John A. Washington, Abraham Buford, Edmund W. Pettus, Theodrick "Tod" Carter, John B. Womack, John H. Winder, Gideon J. Pillow, States Rights Gist, Henry R. Jackson, John Lawton Seabrook, John C. Breckinridge, Leonidas Polk, Zachary Taylor, Sarah Knox Taylor (first wife of Jefferson Davis), Richard Taylor, Davy Crockett, Daniel Boone, Meriwether Lewis (of the Lewis and Clark Expedition) Andrew Jackson, James K. Polk, Abram Poindexter Maury (founder of Franklin, TN), Zebulon Vance, Thomas Jefferson, Edmund Jennings Randolph, George Wythe Randolph (grandson of Jefferson), Felix K. Zollicoffer, Fitzhugh Lee, Nathaniel F. Cheairs, Jesse James, Frank James, Robert Brank Vance, Charles Sidney Winder, John W. McGavock, Caroline E. (Winder) McGavock, David Harding McGavock, Lysander McGavock, James Randal McGavock, Randal William McGavock, Francis McGavock, Emily McGavock, William Henry F. Lee, Lucius E. Polk, Minor Meriwether (husband of noted pro-South author Elizabeth Avery Meriwether), Ellen Bourne Tynes (wife of Forrest's chief of artillery, Captain John W. Morton), South Carolina Senators Preston Smith Brooks and Andrew Pickens Butler, and famed South Carolina diarist Mary Chesnut.

Seabrook's modern day cousins include: Patrick J. Buchanan (conservative author), Cindy Crawford (model), Shelby Lee Adams (Letcher Co., Kentucky, photographer), Bertram Thomas Combs (Kentucky's 50th governor), Edith Bolling (wife of President Woodrow Wilson), and actors Andy Griffith, George C. Scott, Robert Duvall, Reese Witherspoon, Lee Marvin, Rebecca Gayheart, and Tom Cruise.

Seabrook's screenplay, *A Rebel Born*, based on his book of the same name, has been signed with acclaimed filmmaker Christopher Forbes (of Forbes Film). It is now in pre-production, and is set for release in 2016 as a full-length feature film. This will be the first movie ever made of Nathan Bedford Forrest's life story, and as a historically accurate project written from the Southern perspective, is destined to be one of the most talked about Civil War films of all time.

Born with music in his blood, Seabrook is an award-winning, multi-genre, BMI-Nashville songwriter and lyricist who has composed some 3,000 songs (250 albums), and whose original music has been heard in film (*A Rebel Born, Cowgirls 'n Angels, Confederate Cavalry, Billy the Kid: Showdown in Lincoln County, Vengeance Without Mercy, Last Step, County Line, The Mark*) and on TV and radio worldwide. A musician, producer, multi-instrumentalist, and renown performer—whose keyboard work has been variously compared to pianists from Hargus Robbins and Vince Guaraldi to Elton John and Leonard Bernstein—Seabrook has opened for groups such as the Earl Scruggs Review, Ted Nugent, and Bob Seger, and has performed privately for such public figures as President Ronald Reagan, Burt Reynolds, Loni Anderson, and Senator Edward W. Brooke. Seabrook's cousins in the music business include: Johnny Cash, Elvis Presley, Billy Ray and Miley Cyrus, Patty Loveless, Tim McGraw, Lee Ann Womack, Dolly Parton, Pat Boone, Naomi, Wynonna, and Ashley Judd, Ricky Skaggs, the Sunshine Sisters, Martha Carson, and Chet Atkins.

Seabrook, a libertarian, lives with his wife and family in historic Middle Tennessee, the heart of Forrest country and the Confederacy, where his conservative Southern ancestors fought valiantly against Liberal Lincoln and the progressive North in defense of Jeffersonianism, constitutional government, and personal liberty.

LochlainnSeabrook.com

If you enjoyed this book you will be interested in Mr. Seabrook's other popular Civil War related titles:

☞ EVERYTHING YOU WERE TAUGHT ABOUT THE CIVIL WAR IS WRONG, ASK A SOUTHERNER!
☞ CONFEDERATE FLAG FACTS: WHAT EVERY AMERICAN SHOULD KNOW ABOUT DIXIE'S SOUTHERN CROSS
☞ EVERYTHING YOU WERE TAUGHT ABOUT AMERICAN SLAVERY IS WRONG, ASK A SOUTHERNER!
☞ CONFEDERACY 101: AMAZING FACTS YOU NEVER KNEW ABOUT AMERICA'S OLDEST POLITICAL TRADITION

Available from Sea Raven Press and wherever fine books are sold

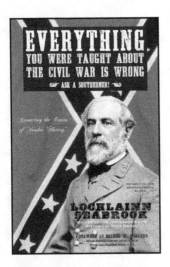

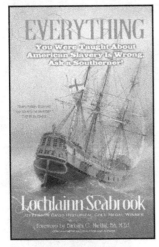

ALL OF OUR BOOK COVERS ARE AVAILABLE AS 11" X 17" POSTERS, SUITABLE FOR FRAMING.

SeaRavenPress.com

CPSIA information can be obtained
at www.ICGtesting.com
Printed in the USA
LVHW030922060821
694091LV00001BA/31